Celebrating the Soul of Cleveland

by Nina Freedlander Gibans

Celebrating the
Soul of Cleveland

by Nina Freedlander Gibans

Text & Original Poetry
Copyright © 2018
by Nina Freedlander Gibans

All other materials remain the intellectual property of the respective originators and are reproduced herein with their permission, and my sincere gratitude.

Cover Design by Jared Bendis
Front Cover Painting *Refuge* by Amy Casey
Back Cover Photograph by Herbert Aschleman, Jr.

ISBN — 9781626130760

Library of Congress Control Number — 2018950676

Published by ATBOSH Media ltd.

Cleveland, Ohio, USA

http://www.atbosh.com

Nina Gibans has long been a force in the cultural life of Cleveland. This book is only one piece, albeit an important one, in her enduring legacy.

Peter Knox, Director
Baker-Nord Center for the Humanities
Case Western Reserve University

"What is that strange combination of grit and grace that makes up 'the soul of Cleveland'?"

It is a question that is especially germane these days as America struggles to comprehend the precipitous fall and phoenix-like revival of its rust-belt cities. The experiment that is America may be concentrating on the coastal media centers, but the real re-invention is taking place in Pittsburgh, Buffalo, Detroit... and Cleveland. Dedicated contemporary populations are building on the history and infrastructure and physical setting of their home cities to re-imagine their city, each city in its own way. Nina Gibans give us her take on what makes Cleveland unique through her own journey through Cleveland past and present. And by connecting the dots and tracing the trajectory, we get a sense of where it is going and what it could be. This is a portrait of Cleveland as only Nina, its most dedicated chronicler, could paint it.

Grafton Nunes
President & CEO
The Cleveland Institute of Art

Author. Poet. Teacher. Catalyst for change. Nina Freedlander Gibans has spent her life working in and advocating for the arts. She is a powerful force in the community—promoting art and artists through her scholarship, passionate activism, and commitment to education. She continues to inspire new generations through word and deed. With her latest project, *Celebrating the Soul of Cleveland*, Nina once again adds to the creative conversation. We are delighted—and grateful—that she is sharing her vision for our city through poetry, storytelling, and wonderfully chosen works of art.

William M. Griswold
Director and President
The Cleveland Museum of Art

This work may look like a simple volume of text and photography, but it is no more that than its author is just another writer. Nina Freedlander Gibans is an unparalleled genius when it comes to weaving together the threads of life—be they ideas, places, people, or poems—into the fabric that makes a community. She brings people together to celebrate the places we share, as this volume connects the ideas and character that inhabit those places. This is a how-to manual, teaching us to love our city, through vision, poetry, and simply paying attention.

Dan Moulthrop
Chief Executive Officer
The City Club of Cleveland

TABLE OF CONTENTS

Acknowledgements	9
Dedication	11
Publisher's Note	13
Preface	15
Prologue	39
Introduction	43
Chapter 1:	47
What is Sustainability?	
Chapter 2:	65
Influences — Mentors — Next Generations	
Chapter 3:	91
Education Ourselves and a Community	
Chapter 4:	107
Greening Our Spirit	
Chapter 5:	119
Cornerstones: Physical and Spiritual	
Chapter 6:	167
Our Collectables:	
Sustaining Our Immediate Environment	
Chapter 7:	213
Affect and Effect	
Epilogue	223
Appendices	229
End Notes	235
Addendum:	247
Voices from the Community	
List of Poems	268
About the Author	271

Acknowledgements

Supporters:
    Anonymous
    Linda and Jack Lissauer

This book, based on unique experiences and ventures, could not have been accomplished without the support of the Baker-Nord Center for the Humanities, Case Western Reserve University, Michael Schwartz Library at Cleveland State University, The Laura and Alvin Siegal Lifelong Learning Program, the management and residents of Moreland Courts, Sean Waterson, Happy Dog, Dan Moulthrop, CEO of The City Club of Cleveland, Pamela Eyerdam, Cleveland Public Library, and participating presenters and panelists for Soul of Cleveland discussions and programs. Risk-takers all.

This project has received so much love and support both from individuals and cultural organizations that I need to say "Thank You". Every image, poem, or other contribution has been carefully documented and credited. For your permission to include it here, I once again say "Thank You".

With great appreciation to Helen Zakin, Michael Yeager, and Ryan Thomas, whose enthusiasm and abilities made them the perfect project associates. And to Jared Bendis, whose persistence matched mine.

Dedication

To James Gibans

A life soulmate

To CAN Magazine whose excellence and dedication to inclusion inspires sustainability into the future.

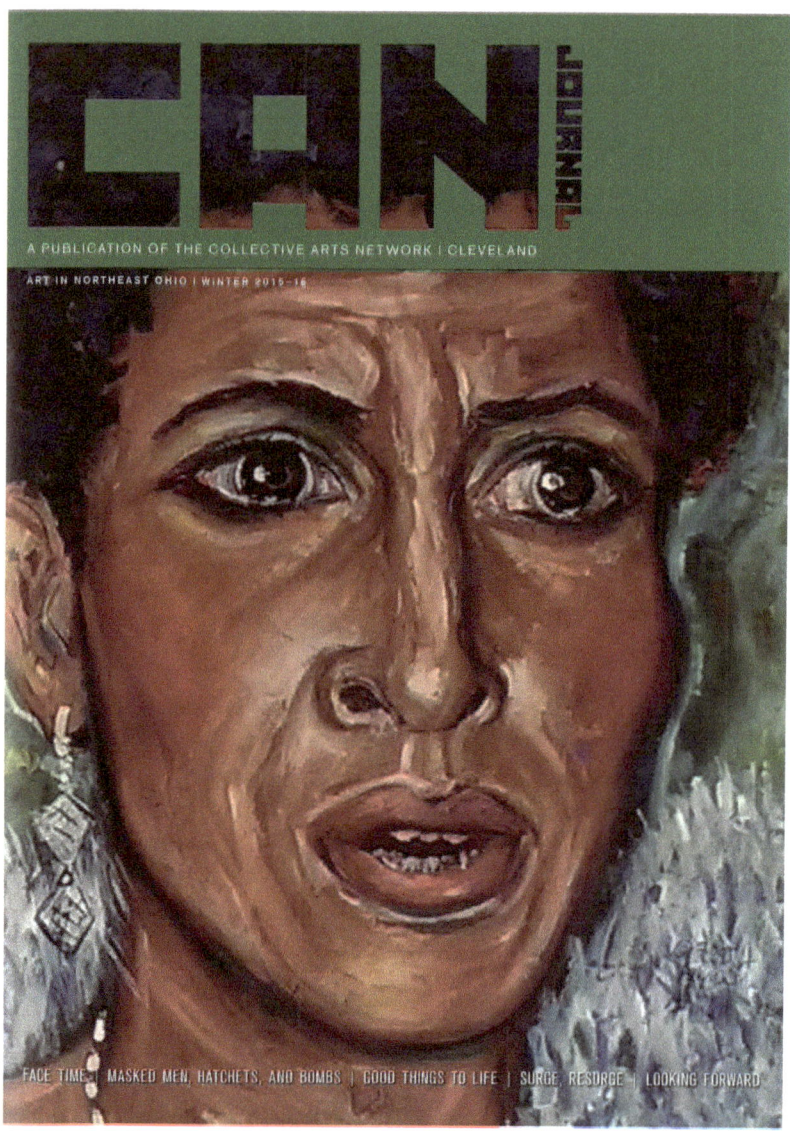

CAN Journal, Winter 2015, Cover Artist: Anna Arnold
Courtesy of the Collective Arts Network

Publisher's Note

As the publisher (and editor) of this book I need to explain to you — the reader — that Nina Gibans is a force to be reckoned with. It is by sheer force of her will and personality that she makes projects happen. Everyone who knows her already knows this. But if you don't know her...

Nina is a General and we are all her army. Just by reading this, you have become a member of the troop. We march along supporting her vision of spreading the vision — of sharing the vision. She is our flag bearer. And what is her "standard"? Well that's the thing, Nina has a multitude of visions but they all appear to come together to celebrate this thing she calls "The Soul of Cleveland".

When I told Nina that I referred to her as a General she replied in a very demure tone, "I would say I am more like a conductor and you all members of the orchestra." And that really is how Nina sees us, organizing our talents to a common goal.

However, to me she will always be the General!

People keep asking me about the book and I tell them it is an epic poem containing stories, ideas, poems and literally hundreds of images of art and artists from Cleveland and beyond. But it is more than that; it is a swirl of text & image, sights, sounds, tastes, and experiences. In it, she attempts to capture and share with you "The Soul of Cleveland".

Jared Bendis

Preface

The Soul of Cleveland project started with a series of discussions at our home... a celebration of our 60 years of marriage and interaction within the community that has molded our lives—our careers, our pleasures, our contacts, our platform for living. For four months, thoughtful folks from many perspectives gathered around our table to discuss the ways in which our community, our environment, this city has made a difference in our lives. They were from the worlds of art, education, architecture and planning, writing and publishing, owners of a bakery, papermaking conservancy, and bookstore. No agendas — focus on the subject. The rich results: a unique survey for community participation, a bibliography full of poetry and books that had influenced them, CDs, and a unique event at the popular Happy Dog restaurant sponsored by Case Western Reserve University. The sessions and the event were captured for anyone interested via internet links. There have been additional events turning unknowns into new stories for today's audiences. The salons have turned into ongoing individual discussions and community events and the surveys have an eternal life and distribution. The subjects, stories and anecdotes are the substance of the Soul of Cleveland. Enlarging them is the provenance of the reader – the hope is to trigger ***their*** version and perspective; they are bound to illuminate and enliven. Almost every conversation has.

Original Freedlander Store in Wooster, OH, now City Steakhouse

Current marker on building that replaced the Freedlander Department Store in 2010.

The Happy Dog on Detroit Avenue. Location of our first session for The Soul of Cleveland. Photograph courtesy of The Happy Dog.

At the Happy Dog Saloon, the first public event moderated by Dan Moulthrop, CEO, The City Club of Cleveland, the Soul of Cleveland program included presentations, visuals, readings entitled "Digging History", "Water, Water Everywhere — Save it", "Save the City", "The Idea Garage of Edwin Mieczkowski"; "Daniel Thompson —Poet Laureate of Cuyahoga County"; "The Physical Soul — Architecture", and the "Old Arcade and By Hand — our ethnic roots".

The following events explored the history of bookstores, multiple-family buildings, varieties of urban farming and aspects of model integration here. All part of our lives.

Family gathering at peak time in Vermont, 2016

Jon Gibans on top of Mount Everest

Beth Gibans with her sustainable project at The Land Institute, from the front page of *The New York Times*.

During our family celebration of this landmark anniversary, eighteen family members –all living outside of this city, traveled by bus together to Akron and Wooster Ohio to trace our family history. A 101-year-old cousin, the first baby born at the now-destroyed Mt. Sinai hospital joined the group in Wooster. The highlights included where Jim lived, went to school and worked, and the Freedlander family who anchored in Wooster in the 1860s (when the horse died, so the story goes). The family stories start back before the Civil War when the Gibansky group merged in Akron. The Freedlanders were an awesome bunch: seven brothers and sisters, two of whom stayed to manage the anchor Freedlander store until 1990. Five moved to Cleveland for high school and higher education, and spawned the first woman Ph.D. at the New School in NYC; the inventors of synthetic rubber and the surgery to eradicate tuberculosis, and the author of the legislation to allow HMOs in Ohio only the tip of their impressive careers. This history deserves its own documentation, the foundation of which is at the Western Reserve Historical Society, and the Wooster Public Library.

Portrait of David Freedlander by Michael Nachtrieb,
Wooster-based artist who also painted Abraham Lincoln.
The artist was paid in booze.

A genealogist in Oregon has become interested in this family history to the point of digging up David Freedlander's passport of 1898 when he tried to recover from illness and died!

This publication will "connect the dots" of unique lives within this community. The list of people who provide the stories and experiences work in and outside of the major and many minor organizations and are the yeast of the bread maker whose immigrant staff models the cultural exchanges that take place among us daily, no matter where we are from: our values, the details of our everyday lives and the expressions of them.

Sustainability in a lifetime is about our heads and hearts; those things that make a difference—the influences, the experiences, our interactions and responses. For each person the confluence creates opportunities to risk, fail and succeed. It challenges us every day to work well with others, meet daily demands that may make us interesting and meet our own potential along the way. It opens doors for progress on our own terms. For us, that is what 60 years have given us.

The Metaphors for our "Soul" — The City as Home–Foundations (streets, waterways, bridges, Stopping Places, Places for Exploring Meanings for ourselves, the meaning of sustenance) One might say that Soul is the Essence of Feeling. Of seeing, of hearing, of form, of our nature and nature around us — of being.

THE SOUL OF CLEVELAND

The Gibans had a 60th anniversary in 2015. Celebrating in our favorite form – discussion – we had Gibans gatherings once a month (about 4-6) at the Gibans home, a coming together of 4-8 people who started by identifying *one thing* (book, work of art, or experience) that influenced the way they saw things, looked at the world, related to others, or allowed them to grow. The result is a publication called "Celebrating the Soul of Cleveland" being published by ATBOSH Media Ltd. These folks are not all in the arts but everyone will know someone in the group.

At meetings in January through June 2015, we shared a non-tangible "essence," a time when all elements had come together and made sense. We had some discussion about what resonated with everyone. The result was a bibliography, a survey distributed to about 1000 people, and an event September 21 at the Happy Dog on 5801 Detroit Avenue under the aegis of the Baker Nord Center for the Humanities at CWRU. In one word, it was a "blast" with a full house. (See attachments for the survey and event program.) The surveys have been a way to involve audiences and will continue to be used.

ORIGINAL GROUP: Suzanne DeGaetano, Michael Gill, Nancy King Smith, Sabine Kretzschmar, Don Harvey, Rick Ortmeyer, Christopher Diehl, Terry Schwarz, Nancy Myrnyack, Jack Bialosky Jr., Ann Klotz and Dan Moulthrop.

COMPONENTS: Bibliography and list of CD and DVDs under ongoing development. SURVEY FOR EVERYONE. Podcast and visuals from the event available. The event used readings and visuals around the stories. People especially liked the inclusion of ethnicity.

THE SOUL OF CLEVELAND
1st Round: September 21, 2015

Sponsored by The Baker-Nord Center for the Humanities, Case Western Reserve University and The City Club of Cleveland.

INTRODUCTORY REMARKS
Peter Knox, Director of the Baker-Nord Center for the Humanities, Case Western Reserve University and Moderator **Dan Moulthrop,** CEO of The City Club of Cleveland.

PROLOGUE
Nina Gibans, Coordinator. "Setting the Stage; Connecting the Dots."

THE SOUL = "Wild Geese" by **Mary Oliver**
Oliver lived here and taught at CWRU (suggested by Rick Ortmeyer). Reader: **David Hassler**, Director of Wick Poetry Center.

THE SOUL = "Digging History"
Art historian and Breadsmith owner **Sabine Kretzschmar**

THE SOUL = "Examining our city from many perspectives since 2000 through urban design research and practice in Cleveland neighborhoods"
Director of the Cleveland Urban Design Collaborative **Terry Schwarz**

THE SOUL = "Water, Water Everywhere – Save it, Save the City"
Victoria Mills, Director, Doan Brook Partnership

THE SOUL = "The Lake Effect"
From *The Hard Way on Purpose* author **David Giffels**

THE SOUL = "People: Edwin Mieczkowski"
Art historian and former assistant of the Putnam Sculpture Collection **Evelyn Kiefer-Roulet**

THE SOUL = "The Physical Soul of Cleveland"
Architects **Jim Gibans & Jennifer Coleman**

THE SOUL = "By Hand – Our Ethnic Roots"
Sabine Kretzschmar on bread making

THE SOUL = "The Future"
Collectors **John Farina** and **Adam Tully**

THE AUDIENCE

CONCLUSIONS: "It was a blast! More, more!"

2nd Round: 4 sessions
Fridays in April from 2-3:30 p.m.
Moreland Courts. Spring 2016

Dubbed "the youngest hippies' and community faculty," Nina Gibans has taught in the community formally and informally for over 50 years. Nina's website is the quickest way to learn out the expertise behind this project.

Sponsors
The Laura and Alvin Siegal Lifelong Learning Program

Session I – *Friday, April 1* – The Soul of Laukhuff, Publix, Loganberry, Coventry Books and Mac's Backs. Bookstores are the backbone of community learning. Anecdotes, focus, variations and visuals, readings.

Session II – *Friday, April 8* – The Soul of the High-Rises – Lakeview Terrace, Moreland Courts and Shaker Towers. Distinguished buildings with important stories. Storytellers, visuals of McVey sculptures and film. [Nina and Jim Gibans are 30-year residents of Shaker Towers and in charge of renovations at Lakeview Terrace, honored early public housing in Cleveland with lifelong residents of Moreland Courts.]

Session III – *Friday, April 15* – The Soul of Our Arcades: Shaker Square and the Old Arcade. Visuals, histories, film. [Gibans have both worked at the old Arcade and both have been on the SHAD board.] The Old Arcade is noted for its structure–one of three in the 1890s worldwide. Shaker Square is the second oldest outdoor shopping mall in the country.

Session IV – *Friday, April 22* – The Soul of Creation with Paper and Book-Preservation. Samples, discussion of Cleveland and focus on papermaking and the importance of publications and preservation. Morgan Conservancy and Strong Bindery.

3rd Round: Greening the City
Happy Dog at Euclid Tavern
Fall 2016

Coming from different perspectives but similar values, the panelists discussed their green "passions", how they have sustained them and us. Henry Doll gardens at his Van Aken Blvd home and delivers zucchinis by bike. His dahlias adorn the tables at FIRE. He heads the Master Garden group at the City Greenhouse. Donita Anderson has awed us all with the growth of the North Union Farmers Markets all over the region including downtown Public Square. Thousands of Clevelanders make it their weekly ritual to shop local and eat healthy from the produce. Noelle Celeste put it all in context out of her experience editing a delicious publication EDIBLE CLEVELAND magazine. David Young, Cleveland Arts Prize poet read from his book, *Seasoning: A Poet's Year: With Seasonal Recipes.*

Moderator, Nina Freedlander Gibans

Sessions like this have been held at area libraries, Nighttown, The Happy Dog, the College Club, Churches, and in residences.

These images were shown as exemplars of the different aspects of the Soul of Cleveland:

Photography of Shaker Lakes from "Preserving Our Natural Heritage", *Shaker Life*, Feb/Mar 2012, by Caydie Heller. Photograph courtesy of *Shaker Life*.

Randall Tiedman, *Night's Speechless Carnival*, 2010. Photograph courtesy of WGS Productions. One of the most poignant depictions of our waterfront.

"And if, like Tiedman in his paintings, you...withdraw to a greater height, it becomes clear that the most important view by far, from Collinwood or anywhere else in northern Ohio, is Lake Erie, which shears off all other geographic features and human doings like a titanic guillotine. You may forget that they're there, yet no more than five blocks from the Grovewood house, the gray waters loom almost secretly, out of all proportion to daily like, as improbable as Leviathan. Mostly hidden from view either by buildings or the lay of the land, the lake is the priceless dreamtime of the city, cradling actual and imaginary worlds in the same primordial gesture, never to be landlocked or subdivided. Its presence in Tiedman's paintings is perhaps the crucial way in which he tells the secret truth of place, a secret, which his images so compellingly argue. We realize that the fundament of Tiedman's tragically peaking and crashing visions isn't earth at all, but water. Paintings like..."Night's Speechless Carnival" (2010) have sometimes been tagged post-apocalyptic, but a close look hints at sources in the Book of Genesis rather than the Book of Revelation. These are places half-drowned and overturned by a great flood." —From Douglas Max Utter's essay "In the Valley of the Shadow" on Tiedman's work at a posthumous retrospective.

Douglas Max Utter, *Cleveland Rain*, 2000 Oil on canvas, 8' x 9'. Photograph courtesy of the artist.

"The painting I call Cleveland Rain...was completed in a downtown studio that overlooked the highway. My picture shows that road, with a bridge and a cloud and a factory building. Unseen behind these lonely-looking commonplaces of the city landscape is another subject, which is my mother's death. I finished the painting in the summer of that year, and she died just at the end of the fall. Her wonderful spirit lives on in many things that she loved and accomplished, and I hope also in this painting." —Douglas Max Utter

William McVey Sculptures at Lakeview Terrace.
Jim Gibans's renovation project.

Lakeview Terrace Playground original from Herman Gibans Fodor Architects Inc. project. The project was reviewed by Lewis Mumford.

Rockefeller Park Bridge, designed by Charles Schweinfurth.
Photography courtesy of the Library of Congress, LC-D4-70782.

Eleanor Roosevelt visiting Lakeview Terrace in 1937
Original from Herman Gibans Fodor Architects Inc. project.

The Old Arcade, Cleveland Memory Project, Cleveland State University, Michael Schwartz Library Special Collections. Referred to by Jennifer Coleman in the "CityProwl Cleveland" podcast.

Daniel Thompson commemorative plaque.

West 2nd Street — now Daniel's Way.
Photograph courtesy of Anthony Hiti.

Laila Voss, *A Chaotic Symphony: The Catch-All Net*, 1996. This image shows a view of the installation at SPACES. 12' x 15' x 17'. Audio, video, 4" television, boom box, 55-gallon drums, roadside debris. Photograph courtesy of the artist.

Laila Voss, *A Chaotic Symphony: The Catch-All Net*, 1996. This image shows a view of the installation at the Cleveland Museum of Art: 15' x 22' x 22'; audio, video, two 4" televisions, bucket planters with weeds, Lake Erie and Cuyahoga River water, nets, 55-gallon drums. Photograph courtesy of the artist.

Laila Voss, *A Chaotic Symphony: The Catch-All Net*, 1996

Three installations for MOCA Cleveland, Cleveland Museum of Art, SPACES for Urban Evidence, Contemporary Artists reveal Cleveland. This image is of the installation at MOCA in which all the compiled and edited sights and sounds of Cleveland were included. App. 25'H x 24'W x 44'L. Construction netting, cable, pallets, tires, taconite, limestone, slag, reprocessed steel scrap, coke, recycled G.E. glass, 30-gallon drums, weeds, four LCD monitors, two Walkmans, two boom boxes, four separate audio tracks, six separate videos. Photographs courtesy of the artist.

Michelangelo Lovelace *78th Street and Nowhere* 1994 Shown at Happy Dog event, September 2015.

Edwin Mieczkowski, *Blue and White Ford*, 1966
Acrylic on canvas, 47 5/8" x 41 7/16"
This was the artist's favorite painting.

Installation view of work by Jared Åkerström for the exhibition Formulated Play" at Survival Kit, 2014. Laser-cut polyester terephthalate (PETG), aluminum hardware, spray-paint, and wooden frame. Photography courtesy of John Farina and Adam Tully.

Samuel Oscar Freedlander

Verb Ballet at Cain Park, 2017.
Photograph courtesy of Bill Naiman.

Verb Ballet at Cain Park.
Photograph courtesy of Bill Naiman.

Prologue

We have sat on the grass at Cain Park and Blossom, in the dutiful seats of many school auditoria, the semi-cushy ones in renewed venues, the plushy one at Severance Hall and the Cleveland Museum of Art healing our bruised derrieres. We have entered open spaces, spaces via thin make-do curtains, and opened heavy bronze doors. We have thrown ourselves to the wind and sun at the empty beaches, the metro-parks, architected and historic homes on the Erie shore to inhale the essence of water and bright sky, grey sky and sand. I know we have been to every gallery in town. We open our snail mail and e-mail daily to keep informed and to decide what to explore.

We have recently been sustained and moved by:

- The joy of an icon of childhood given a permanent home at the Western Reserve Historical Society of the Euclid Beach Grand Park CAROUSEL after 45 years and about two decades of dedication from those who cared enough.

- The joy of following David Beach's 'eco-bucket list' of 10 ecological experiences that can change behavior — his bioregional education.
- The joy of the number of institutions that have had enormous impact over the last 60-100 years, including the City Club of Cleveland, The Cleveland Orchestra, The Cleveland Institute of Art, Laurel School. Hawken School, the Cleveland Museum of Art, The Cleveland Public Library system, Cuyahoga County Library system, and Independent Libraries such as Shaker Heights Public Library, Cleveland Heights Public Library.
- The joy of Viktor Schreckengost who taught how to observe people especially children in action, something almost forgotten.
- The joy of the Metroparks and every green space we can hug.
- The joy of the impact of our systems of philanthropy and their visions.
- The joy of the caring and serving of people needing food and life-supplies of support exampled by the Food Bank and Community Gardens.
- The joy of the new numbers of people enjoying the benefits of partnered programs among organizations.
- The up-beat energy around the city in anticipation of a bright and significant future as anchored and important as that of those who have worked to make it that way.

This reflects only today's mail in the Gibans household. We have heard from all of them.

This book is about sharing those experiences that have made Cleveland a place that has kept us open to new perception and understanding about this city over the 80 years that we've been here and the 60 years that we've shared it.

Severance Hall.
Photography courtesy of Roger Mastroianni.

Montessori High School at University Circle, located on Magnolia Drive. Building by Charles Schweinfurth and renovated by Jim Gibans.

Introduction

Pablo Neruda's *Book of Questions* was required reading wherever and whenever I have taught **because he jolted our thinking, wonderment, imagination, creativity and said "be yourself"**. The Gibans have shared some renewed discussion of his magic. These thoughts are the basis for writing this book on the sustainability of life in Cleveland. The resonance.

One person recently labeled us the oldest "hippies"; another said Nina was "faculty to the community". Could be? Nina was a street poet in San Francisco during the "beat era" and has taught formally or produced programs at Capital University, Cleveland State University, Case Western Reserve University, The Cleveland Museum of Art, The Cleveland Public Library, the Cuyahoga County Library and Independent Library Systems, Greater Cleveland Growth Association and many less formal settings such as The Happy Dog Saloon and Moreland Courts, the iconic multi-residential facility at Shaker Square. Architect Jim has his own stations in City Hall, Cleveland, Lakeview Terrace, the early Public Housing Complex, and the Montessori High School at University Circle. They've been a team throughout life. This book is about these adventures — experiences and participations and accompanying perceptions and observations. Here are stories heard loudly or never heard before. They have affected our lives and those of this community and are organized to illuminate the expanded definition of sustainability, its relationship to influences, mentors and next generations, educating ourselves and a community, the meaning of "green", cornerstones and the physical environment, our collectables, and the affect and effect of this 60 years.

Amy Casey, *Refuge*, 2015 Acrylic on panel, 8" x 10"
Nina and Jim Gibans Collection Honoring their 60th anniversary
Also the cover of this book!

Dale Eldred, *Light Path Crossing*, 1987 Case Western Reserve University. Children looked for the sun shining on this piece on their way to the Cleveland Children's Museum as a special spotlight.

Between the Erie Canal and rivers running north to the big Lake Erie, lies the story of a woodland-turned city, a piece of land between the trails to Buffalo and Detroit, between the rambling frame and the elegant eclectic European-style buildings, reflective of the post-Civil War industrial haven born and grown by self-made leaders hungry to win "their" Midwest. Those leaders saw their vision grow into the green lands of the metropolitan and national parks (Emerald necklace and Cuyahoga Valley National Park), inland lakes (Shaker Lakes and Doan Brook connections) and the decade-old Canal Towpath project, and newly dreamed Red Line greenway. We can stow away at lunchtime at the pocket parks (Eastman Garden) or sit on the historic bench at Jacob Field. We were born in the depression, our families saw the city blossom, watched it thrive and languish, almost expire, and rise with renewed energy today connecting the new-timers and the old-timers. We are the last of our 2-generation immigrant families living in this region.

Angelica Pozo and Penny Rakoff, *Marketplace/Meetingplace: An Urban Memorial*, 18" x 25' x 7', Concrete, ceramic mosaic, ceramic relief sculpture & historic artifacts. A poignant tribute to the history of Cleveland's market district, located outside Jacob's Field Ballpark.

Chapter 1:
What is Sustainability?

The lilacs, the bridges, the street corners, the lakes, the public spaces, the cozy settings, the food, the roses, the caregivers and caretakers, our personal heroes, music, visual art in all forms, dance, movement, books, buildings, design and form, food: experiences that have changed our perspective. When we talk of a sustainable world, we tend to think globally—about things that are almost beyond our individual control. We forget some of the things that affect us personally. They surround us; are they the poetry of our lives?

Lilac Lane — at Euclid and Martin Luther King. A favorite memory of Nina's. Image 00814, Case Western Reserve University Archives.

Athena Tacha's *Merging*, 1985-86 8' x 71' x 83' ft., Stepped pyramidal waterfall sculpture constructed of poured concrete sheathed in blue and red granite. See what the John Hay High School students have to say about this piece in the film "University Circle: Creating a Sense of Place".

Sustainability

Sustainability
Greens the imagination
Sunrise of ideas
Awakens slumbering memories
Each of us has a field of ground cover
Hovering over the fruits of tomorrow
Where we come from; what we are this day.
I am curious what I will remember
A lavender dance wafts its way
From Lilac Lane that disappeared when I looked away
To smell the roses on the table each summer
And of Blood Wedding's ribbons of red for my ripped heart.
And the grey of this city's backdrop.

—NFG

The Metaphors for our "Soul" set the stage for a community wide survey. It went like this:

We asked people wherever we went: waiters, walkers, shoppers, neighbors, friends, and audiences — invading some thoughts in the aisles of theaters, grocery stores, and passing on the sidewalks to answer the community survey. Here are the questions, some replies and thoughts as we gravitate among them.

What is a childhood memory about Cleveland to share?

Over and under bridges. Echoes. Sound. The joy of play. Honking our horn under the beautiful strong yet gentle bridges over Rockefeller Park, one of the most gracious drives in the city. Then Sunday after Sunday crossing the river and standing next to the engineer turning the swing bridge over the Cuyahoga, watching him make it straight so we could cross over My father doing rounds at City Hospital gave my sister and me a ride to remember.

What aspects of the city had the highest impact? What stories needed to be preserved or be lost to the present and future. Stories need documentation not only for the record of how people perceive but for their civic value. Every generation needs to have the opportunity of knowing about important civic moments of all kinds. They need to make sense in a context and need repetition for each generation.

The group decided on these questions. We are still gathering answers.

The Soul of Cleveland Survey
The questions and the top answers

1. When someone from out of town visits, where do you take them if they want to experience the "real" Cleveland?

- Cleveland Museum of Art

What will we explore today, any day — teach ourselves, each other? Just look. The Frank Gehry building across University Circle expands the concept of sculpture gray glistening in the sun in frozen waves against a sky that matches.

- West Side Market

Honor ethnic heritage. Smell the fresh-baked pastries, admire whole fish, watch aproned grocers wring handmade sauerkraut or swirl peanut butter. A hour-long tasting party or self-determined snack.

- Downtown

The heart of nostalgia — creative department store windows especially at holidays — window-shopping before catalogs – Mayor Tom Johnson respected and mentioned — and the –Soldiers and Sailors Monuments — Lessons in local history worth getting to know and visiting before catching the bus. Lots of new green space to look forward to.

- Severance Hall (Cleveland Orchestra)

Hands down, a favorite building. Elegant, eclectic, jaw-dropping gold details, a ceiling and stage our platform for a lifetime of mostly perfect sound.

- University Circle

Walk around; explore a moving civic transformation, something from all time to this day to celebrate. With 54 cultural, education and heath institutions, how can we miss? The beautiful old of Magnolia Drive and the ever-changing Euclid Avenue bookend the green spaces for ice-skating, parading and lying in the grass looking at the sky.

- Little Italy

Still a well-preserved enclave reminiscent of ethnic neighborhoods created to house the workers who built the railroads, worked as stone carvers and taught us how to play Bocce ball. The Old Schoolhouse a favorite spot housing artists and boutique shopping.

- Ohio City

The West Side's early gentrification – folks fixing family places, new restaurants and finally a BIG market. Cozy, city living on the edge of the Gordon Arts district still developing with theatres, movies, and energy.

People find comfort in many places; we take our guests where their interest tells us to explore one place or another. We try to include the bridges over Rockefeller Park, the Flats, and west side venues, especially the modern houses facing the Lake at W 64th street which are a favorite spot for watching fourth of July fireworks.

2. Who is your favorite Cleveland villain?
- Art Modell
- Danny Greene
- Sam Shepard
- LeBron James * (switch to hero June 2016)
- Cleveland Police Force
- Shondor Birns
- Albert Porter

If Albert Porter had gotten his way, the Clark Freeway would have sliced the area between Shaker Square and Warrensville-no more Shaker Heights. He was not to get his way!

3. Who is your favorite Cleveland hero?
- Superman
- Carl Stokes
- Elliott Ness
- LeBron James
- Amanda Berry
- Michael Symon
- Peter B. Lewis

The city needs more visionaries like Peter B. Lewis who pushed for change at Case Western Reserve University stimulating much that happened in the next decades to place it among top Ohio Universities. And, the Gehry building.

4. What is Cleveland's/NE Ohio's best kept secret?
   - Wade Chapel in Lakeview Cemetery
   - The wonderful music and art that is so outstanding and accessible.
   - We have water. As the rest of the country dries up, we will control the water.
   - Big Al's Diner — best corned beef hash and diverse crowd of people in business suits, uniforms. Sunday Brunch folks fill this storefront on Larchmere without pause after 10 am.
   - Cuyahoga Valley Towpath
   - All the wonderful ethnic food
   - I am

All of the mentioned secrets sustain our life in special ways from the old-fashioned diner and ethic food spots to the hard-fought-for towpath marking important history. Water became a main discussion for the group around the table.

5. What is your favorite body of water in Cleveland?
   - Lake Erie
   - Cuyahoga River
   - Doan Brook
   - Chagrin River
   - Horseshoe Lake
   - Wade Lagoon

There is a romanticism and splendor about the Shaker Lakes, the story of their preservation and development down to Lake Erie known as the Doan Brook Partnership Project = "Save our Water, Save our City"

6. Where is your favorite place to view it?
   - From a boat
   - From a window of Special Collections at CPL
   - Terminal Tower Observation Deck
   - The Cleveland Flats
   - Mentor Headlands
   - Edgewater
   - The bridge over the Falls
   - On the steps in front of CMA
   - Along the shorelines

7. What other ways do you engage with it?
   - Visit sites, buildings, programs, take walks
   - Stand up paddle boarding, sea kayaking, Nautica, fishing
   - Spend time near it at various attractions
   - I like to sit by the water
   - I stay away after almost drowning in it
   - Work and live a walk away — truly a pleasure
   - I get seasick, so I like it from the ground. It looks beautiful from the top of the Garfield Monument.
   - Explore shorelines for nooks and crannies, inlets, stones and shells; pick a spot for painting or fishing there.

8. What is your favorite street?
    - Fairmount Boulevard
    - Lakeshore Boulevard
    - MLK
    - East Boulevard
    - Euclid Avenue
    - Larchmere Boulevard
    - Coventry
    - South Park Boulevard
    - Magnolia Drive at University Circle and the drive through Rockefeller Park

9. Where is the best place to have a conversation?
    - Any friend's backyard (summer). Any friend's living room (winter).
    - At the Lagoon of the Cleveland Museum of Art.
    - At one of the many wonderful coffee shops in Cleveland.
    - Dewey's at Shaker Square
    - Rockefeller's
    - Cleveland Museum of Art courtyard
    - Luna Café
    - Around our table or in a comfortable chair.

10. What is your favorite "festival"?
    - Cleveland International Film Festival
    - Summer Solstice at CMA
    - Parade the Circle
    - Ingenuity Festival
    - Hessler Street Fair
    - Feast of the Assumption
    - Cain Park Arts Festival

- Parade the Circle

True participation, no motorized floats, bumblebees, stilt walkers moving to their own beat. Creative minds and communities within communities spinning their best ideas. The sun has performed as well most years enhancing color and smiles most years. Ethnic festivals bring heritage to performances, costumes. Greek, Italian, and the newer Dyngus Day celebrated in Poland and Buffalo on the Monday after Easter when accordions make the day ring truer than just "milling and eating".

11. What is your favorite outdoor concert venue?
    - Blossom
    - Transformer Station
    - Wade Oval
    - Nautica
    - Cain Park

The one with the best program. Cain Park for Dance and Musicals—sat almost on top of the stage for The King and I and way back for Apollo's Fire in folk guise. Groundworks trying new choreography and we are literally sitting on top of the stage. During a thunderstorm at Blossom, the orchestra never missed a glorious beat. Wade Oval ice skating brings back earlier afternoons at the Elysium. The Transformer Station feels new on the wall and outside.

12. What is your favorite building in NE Ohio?
    - Severance Hall
    - Cleveland Museum of Art
    - West Side Market
    - Terminal Tower
    - Van Sweringen Mansion
    - Cleveland Trust Building
    - The Old Arcade
    - Peter B. Lewis Building

Severance Hall with its jaw-dropping renovation and beautiful interior. The Cleveland Museum of Art's renovation and expansion and the Frank Gehry building create very special environments.

13. What is your favorite restaurant?
    - Johnny's Downtown
    - Table 45
    - Fire at Shaker Square
    - Night Town
    - Mama Catena's
    - Larchmere Tavern
    - Academy Tavern
    - Sokolowski's

Depends how hungry you are and how much money you have. One of the best birthday parties was at the Academy Tavern — a guest happy with the first restaurant breakfast meal served hot.

14. Where is your favorite place to go for a walk?
    - Shaker Lakes
    - Cleveland Zoo
    - Metroparks
    - University Circle
    - Huntington Beach in Bay Village
    - Edgewater Park
    - Mentor Headlands
    - Cleveland Botanical Gardens
    - How can one choose? Make a point of trying each

Survey Answers – Laura Peskin

1. Where to take out-of-towners:
   - Kiss the piles of sand and what have you in the industrial flats; look up and see the Guardians of Traffic looming above you.
   - Check out our numerous local history museums (Euclid, Bedford, Conneaut, more)
2. Villain: Jimmy Dimora
3. Hero: Judge Raymond Pianka (Superhero: Superman)
4. Secret:
   - Cleveland Lakefront Bike Trail
   - Extant Prehistoric Cleveland: earthen embankments at Greenwood Village, Sag. Hills, CVNP; Fort Hill behind RR Nature Center; Indian Point in Painesville/ Leroy, similar
5. Body of Water: Lake Erie
6. Viewing Lake/ water resources: From Cleveland Lakefront Nature Preserve (Dike 14)
7. Engaging with Lake/ water resources: Watch migratory warblers enjoy the volleyball net in Wendy Park; hang out at Dyer's Deco Coast Guard Station.
8. Favorite Street: Euclid Avenue from downtown to eastern most City of East Cleveland (9 remaining Euclid Ave. mansions/ carriage houses, hidden pre Civil War landmarks in East Cleveland)
9. Conversation: Shaker Lakes
10. Festival: Larchmere Porch Fest
11. Outdoor Concert Venue: bandstand in Bedford Commons (i.e. Pooka)
12. Building: University Circle United Methodist Church (Oilcan)
13. Restaurant: Tommy's
14. Walk: Holden Arboretum

Survey Answers – Betsy Sullivan

1. Favorite Street: W. 25th Street
2. Favorite Street Corner: E. 14th and Euclid Ave. Why? I love the new chandelier and streetscape, the concentration of theaters and restaurants and its walkability and access to so much of the cool new vibe in downtown.
3. Favorite neighborhood: Ohio City
4. Best place for a conversation: Used to be Rising Star Coffee Roasters on W. 29th Street but they'd removed the outdoor seating last time I was there. 2nd choice: Artefino on Superior Ave.
5. Favorite Festival: Cleveland International Film Festival
6. Least Favorite Festival: None. All festivals are good!
7. Favorite outdoor concert venue: Blossom
8. Favorite NE Ohio building: Severance Hall
9. Favorite restaurant: Il Bacio
10. Favorite place for a walk: Cuyahoga Valley National Park
11. Preferred destination for tourists to see "real Cleveland": W. 25th Street
12. Favorite Cleveland villain: Cleveland torso murderer
13. Favorite Cleveland hero: Superman
14. Cleveland/NE Ohio's best-kept secret: Waterfront
15a. Most memorable experience with Lake Erie: Sailing and swimming off sailboat
15b. Most memorable experience with the Cleveland Museum of Art: Visiting the museum with someone whose family had donated the portrait we were viewing.
15c. Most memorable experience with Severance Hall: Sitting on stage because of an overflow crowd at what I believe was a Mstislav Rostropovich solo concert.
16. Favorite body of water in NE Ohio: Lake Erie
17. Favorite place to view it: Looking toward Cleveland over the lake from the end of Lake Park Dr. in Bay Village before a new mammoth home obscured this extraordinary view.
18. Other ways that I engage with Lake Erie: Walks.
19. Childhood memory of Cleveland: I have lived in Cleveland since 1979 and moved here as an adult.

Survey Answers – William Bruner II

1. Favorite Street: Weybridge – lived there 25 years.
2. Favorite Street Corner: Shaker Square – many memories there over 60+ years.
3. Favorite Neighborhood: Shaker Square – grew up there!
4. Best place for a conversation: Dewey's at Shaker Square
5. Favorite Festival: Garlic Festival – Shaker Square
6. Least favorite festival: None.
7. Favorite outdoor concert venue: Blossom
8. Favorite NE Ohio building: Moreland Courts – in family since 1937
9. Favorite restaurant: Fire and Sasa
10. Favorite place for a walk: Shaker Lakes
11. Preferred destination for tourists to see "real Cleveland": Shaker Square, University Circle, & Tower City / Terminal Tower
12. Favorite Cleveland hero: Bob Feller
13. Cleveland/NE Ohio's best-kept secret: Cleveland Museum of Natural History
14a. Most memorable experience with Lake Erie: Boating off of Kelly's Island
14b. Most memorable experience with the Cleveland Museum of Art: Many visits. The new addition.
14c. Most memorable experience with Severance Hall: Many concerts
15. Favorite body of water in NE Ohio: Lake Erie
16. Favorite place to view it: On deck at Moreland Courts
18. Other ways that I engage with Lake Erie: We own a house on Kelly's Island on the water.
19. Childhood memory of Cleveland: Too many to recollect – all good!

Listening

An even dozen takes us East.
Vintage 1930, 1957, 1992.
One with eight brothers and sisters
One an only child
Subcultures picking through childhood traditions
Chocolate brownies, great grandmother's butterscotch cookies
Best parks for flying kites higher higher, higher
Real Vermont sugar and love.

ERROL GARNER by the sea
Where or When
Stories pulled from shredded
Time — add salt — a little more sugar
A week of tales just for us.

BENNY GOODMAN on the radio
Moving through our dance
Hands air-beating rhythms
Humming long ago and now
Fresh as a corsage at the dance
Wilting only in memory.

McCOY TYNER TRIO live at Sweet Basil
Swing
Round Midnight
We are sitting near the music
Drinking it
Now it is the tomorrow
And we are still at the table.

W.A. MOZART in Two Acts
Opera Buffa
Laughing at the details
Never shared quite this way
Too new for telling; too old to remember wholly
This is the perfect moment to try.

ANTONIN DVORAK
Symphonic Poems
Calling to our spirit
Chasing butterflies or fireflies
Racing bikes to roaring falls
Unearthing secrets, vaults and valleys,
Mountain spaces, designed
For peace and contemplation.

HAYDN'S
Great Symphonies Nos 43 — Mercury
E Flat Major on high dirt roads of Morocco
59 in A Major—Fire of Copper Canyon red
Excitement in fast-spinning wheels
Like fast forwarding CDs
Tracks and roads, narrow as ribbons
Glorious wind
Beauty in the dust.

HAYDN's
Piano Sonatas
Nos 29, 31, 34, 35, and 49
Quiet by the stream
Yellow buds poking through the soil
Past green heights past color
Except the white-grey clouds
Complementing the ground.

JOHANN SEBASTIAN BACH-
Musical offering
In our own vaulted space
Splendor of centuries and our 60 years
It is on our alter
As we look at what we have brought
Together.

—NFG

Chapter 2:
Influences — Mentors — Next Generations

Whoever you are, no matter how lonely,
the world offers itself to your imagination,
calls to you like the wild geese, harsh and exciting
over and over announcing your place
in the family of things.

From "Wild Geese" by Mary Oliver

No one escapes many of life's grueling possibilities: accidents, deaths, illnesses, feelings of abandonment, loneliness, financial loss. Part of one's life's responsibilities is struggling against whatever odds you have been given. A two-lb. baby born more than 80 years ago was not supposed to "make it". But I am the last one to carry the family name. I was "feisty", and thrived with the help of attitudes: my father: "Women (even those with cerebral palsy) should follow their passions"; my teachers: allowed me to type with three fingers because my handwriting was so slow; physical therapists helping me to succeed physically and a husband understating and understanding the issues — never standing in the way of progress. With an absence of labels, colleagues, friends, mentors never doubted persistence, a smile, and exciting goals with programs that bettered the community.

So it was when we met around the table on the occasion of 60 years of marriage; *The Soul of Cleveland* was a celebration of relationships, of this supporting community. It was to share the sustainability of a city; soul is about heart and head — about feelings not what we do. For six months, thoughtful folks from many perspectives gathered around our table to discuss *the Soul of Cleveland*, a celebration of relationships and 60 years of marriage. Among them were educators, artists, environmentalists, bookstore owners, writers, architects, historians.

The group started by identifying one thing that had made a difference in their lives — changed their perspective — moved them to better knowing the city or themselves. An architect read "Wild Geese" a poem by Mary Oliver who has inspired poets and people searching for ways to express their souls. She was born in Maple Heights, taught at Case Western Reserve University, and has achieved honor as "visionary" and one of America's finest poets. What an amazing start to our thinking.

Gaston Bauchelard's book *The Poetics of Space* was my offering. I have marked up two copies because it held such valuable ideas of place, of roots, gave me inspiration and comfort. When I went to a 50th reunion at Sarah Lawrence College, we shared one book with our classmates that had made a difference in our lives. This book was mentioned by two of us. In Cleveland, I found that it is a favorite of art history professors and their students. But for me it has inspired poems through the years. David Giffel's book *The Hard Way on Purpose* on growing up in the decaying city of Akron reflected who we are — full of hope on the heels of despair described through interrelationships with people — our friends — and places with meaning. Life is growing through the stuff of teenage, filled with boredom and invented activity and gaining understandings of the meaning of where we are as people and want to be. Giffels use of decaying buildings as platforms for action is memorable. These books and others became the core of the bibliography developed though the months. The section on sustainability establishes what is meaningful to citizens.

"The Hard Way on Purpose" by David Giffels

Others in the group offered stories of simple heroic efforts in Cleveland that signaled community and a sense of caring. In particular, one was about a missing dog and the search by the whole neighborhood until it was found. Another story was about an old woman, worried that a tire in the middle of the road would cause harm, stepped off of the berm of safety to remove it.

Think about influences, families, mentors, teachers, colleagues.

I started to understand some of the challenges of life at Laurel School, where one would have a hard time relating to today with its stellar leadership in the education of young women, and values that resonate democracy, neighborhood, decency, hard work and hard play, and ... Excellence.

My challenges included being the only democrat and Jew in my third grade class, and being pointed to as an example Aryan with blue eyes and blond hair in high school. I was not invited informally to my classmates' homes and was a wallflower at Dancing School. I went on to Wellesley College where I mourned a roommate's suicide. At Sarah Lawrence College, I became responsible for my own "learning" and absorbed the meaning of the McCarthy hearings as editor of the college newspaper by having to handle the results of the congressional hearings to which faculty were subpoenaed. I became a devotee of Arthur Miller, who came to the campus during those times to talk of freedom of speech and education. He had just finished *The Crucible.*

It took about 25 years to reconnect with my Laurel classmates who I still see today, and I have been devoted to classmates from Wellesley and Sarah Lawrence for 60 years.

At Sarah Lawrence, we were expected to map out a path for continuous growth. It was there that we researched, reported, discussed, wrote and delivered. My mentors were mainly in art and literature: William Rubin, later Curator of Painting at MOMA, poets Horace Gregory, Alastair Reid, and Joseph Campbell, the voice for current thinking in philosophy and mythology. Sarah Lawrence College embodied the spirit of collaborative and integrated study. I have carried that philosophy throughout the years and community projects.

"....This is more than a dream;
It is something that is awake
Within a dream; it wakes
    And follows you out of bed,
    Out of the room, out of the house
    And down the street. Hear
    Them through an open window..."

    From "The Cage of Voices" by Horace Gregory

Jim and I met on a blind date through friends of my father and it "worked". He had just graduated from Yale College School of Architecture where his mentors included humanities faculty and leading architects and planners; George Howe, Josef Albers, Vincent Scully, and Philip Johnson.

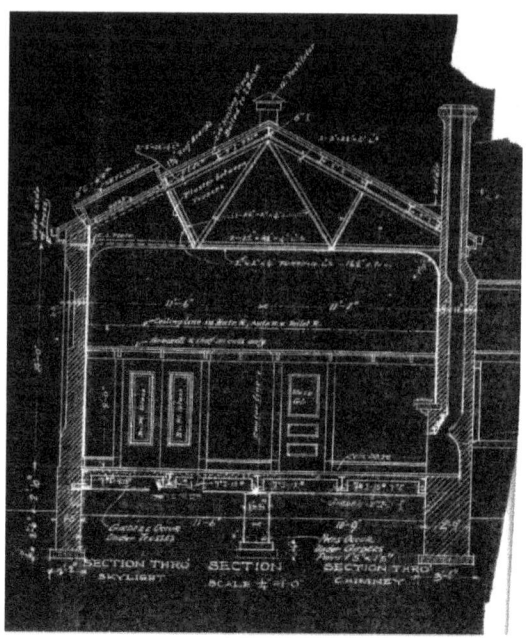

Rowfant drawing done by Jim Gibans.

He had a Fulbright in City Planning in Liverpool and we honeymooned in England, France and Italy. I held the tripod while he took pictures!

Back to Cleveland for real life, Jim was drafted. We started life in Kansas where he was among the last draftees after the Korean War and then went to San Francisco to start his architectural career. We had 4 children under 7; I was a street poet in San Francisco writing with groups at the San Francisco Library and the San Francisco Poetry Center – small, intense, productive sessions with poet Louis Zukofsky and Vincent McHugh, former head of New York City's WPA Writers' project. We wrote a joint poem, read our own in bars, coffee houses and on stage with Allen Ginsberg. We congregated at City Lights, still an iconic bookstore feeding hungry minds. This was the midst of the Beat Era in San Francisco. Talk about timing! These WERE mentors; the time spent with each is significant for understanding myself in the world of poetry. Allen Ginsberg read *Howl* the night our poetry group read our poems as a preliminary "act". That poem and *A Supermarket in California* have stayed with me for their poignancy and enviable choice of images.

A Supermarket in California
Allen Ginsberg

What thoughts I have of you tonight Walt Whitman, for I walked down the sidestreets under the trees with a headache self-conscious looking at the full moon.

In my hungry fatigue, and shopping for images, I went into the neon fruit supermarket, dreaming of your enumerations!

What peaches and what penumbras! Whole families shopping at night! Aisles full of husbands! Wives in the avocados, babies in the tomatoes!—and you, Garcia Lorca, what were you doing down by the watermelons?

I saw you, Walt Whitman, childless, lonely old grubber, poking among the meats in the refrigerator and eyeing the grocery boys.

I heard you asking questions of each: Who killed the pork chops? What price bananas? Are you my Angel?

I wandered in and out of the brilliant stacks of cans following you, and followed in my imagination by the store detective.

We strode down the open corridors together in our solitary fancy tasting artichokes, possessing every frozen delicacy, and never passing the cashier.

Where are we going, Walt Whitman? The doors close in an hour. Which way does your beard point tonight?

(I touch your book and dream of our odyssey in the supermarket and feel absurd.)

Will we walk all night through solitary streets? The trees add shade to shade, lights out in the houses, we'll both be lonely.

Will we stroll dreaming of the lost America of love past blue automobiles in driveways, home to our silent cottage?

Ah, dear father, graybeard, lonely old courage-teacher, what America did you have when Charon quit poling his ferry and you got out on a smoking bank and stood watching the boat disappear on the black waters of Lethe?

Berkeley, 1955

Allen Ginsberg, "A Supermarket in California" from Collected Poems 1947-1980. Copyright © 1984 by Allen Ginsberg. Reprinted with the permission of HarperCollins Publishers, Inc.

Back in Cleveland, I became the last graduate student of Thomas Munro at Case Western Reserve University who taught Art History and Aesthetics from his Cleveland Museum of Art loft. He directed the Education Department of the Museum and edited the *Journal of Aesthetics.* My thesis was on Charles Ives, Winslow Homer and Walt Whitman. I wrote program notes for the Chamber Music Society.

These notes emphasize how fortunate we were to have these academic mentors. Mentors in so many areas of our thought. They have resonated throughout our lives. So have the monthly program notes at Cleveland Cinemateque where one can see films several times a weekend — offerings primarily of the best of the past and peek of the future by the most provocative and talented filmmakers, actors, and directors. The Cleveland International Film Festival where my film, *Creative Essence* was shown in 2003, enhances our perspective of today's filmmaking worldwide. CIFF is a model of a community-based organization with a small year-round staff and hundreds of volunteers and superb leadership. Learning on all levels.

Observing, visiting, working sessions, talking to leaders and artists we learn about risk, change, compatibility, and camaraderie. The stories about these realities sustain us.

Our largest and one of the smallest works in our private art collection were bought at benefits for the Center for Contemporary Art (now MOCA Cleveland). It has been no secret that Cleveland was behind in its understanding and acceptance of contemporary art; serious collectors went elsewhere to make their purchases and followed the national art picture. First, The New Gallery in 1968, then The Center for Contemporary Art in 1984 opened in a storefront almost directly across the street from their current 35 million dollar building, making the Museum of Contemporary Art comparable to peer institutions in Denver, St. Louis and Cincinnati. We learned at their exhibitions, programs and lectures. Jim was the architect for their interim move to the Galleria and I have written critically about their stimulating, risk-taking exhibitions. Cleveland was introduced to art by Andy Warhol, Christo, and Claes Oldenburg, and many others. MOCA continues to bring the work of emerging and established regional, national, and international artists to our area.

Cristo-wrapped New Gallery (now MOCA). Storefront on Euclid Avenue. Nina took Cristo to the airport. Photograph courtesy of MOCA Cleveland. © MOCA Cleveland 2018.

Exhibitions that have resonated with us include the early ones shown in the small storefront gallery on Euclid Avenue and on Bellflower of iconic artists such as

Jasper Johns and Red Grooms, *The Teacher and the Student: Charles Rosenthal and Ilya Kabakov* (2004) from their space in the Play House building on Carnegie Avenue. My pleasure was to drive Christo to the airport just after he had "wrapped" the first gallery storefront and before he "wrapped" Central Park in New York.

SPACES located on viaduct, following several moves from their original home at 1375 Euclid. See weed pot by first director Rob Mihaly.

SPACES, now located on Detroit Avenue. This photograph taken at its groundbreaking on 6/28/16. SPACES conducted a comprehensive capital campaign to purchase and renovate the first floor of the Van Roy Coffee Building (located at 2900 Detroit Avenue). Photograph courtesy of Deidre McPherson.

SPACES has traveled from 1375 Euclid Avenue to the Warehouse District to their home for several years on the aqueduct bridge and are in a new home in Hingetown, near the TRANSFORMER, a renovated art space. Their hope is to connect with the community thoroughly to create a solid neighborhood of residents, small business owners and non-profit arts organizations. This emulates what we experience as residents of the Shaker Square community.

Sustenance during a lifetime in this city: These wonderful mentors — the list grows daily, by phone, e-mail, planned meetings and chance meetings. They are buried and unburied unexpectedly. Usefully, by reference and happenstance. They are friends daily and for life.

>They teach us about looking
>They teach us about color
>They correct expression
>They enhance verbiage
>They hug our minds

Ilya Kabakov's (as Charles Rosenthal), *Charles Rosenthal: Twelve Commentaries on Suprematism #3*, 1926, An Interesting Book, pictured here, is Nina's favorite painting from MOCA.

Installation view of the exhibition: *The Teacher and The Student: Charles Rosenthal and Ilya Kabakov* at the Museum of Contemporary Art Cleveland in 2004. Photograph courtesy of MOCA Cleveland. © MOCA Cleveland 2018.

They encourage ideas and embrace what works. I am still meeting mentors. I met one yesterday and will meet another tomorrow. Because they continue to communicate and enliven my mind, our collaboration of thought is real, alive, and vital. They are the Soul of Cleveland. This week the factual count is 10, from 5 libraries, 2 universities and the neighborhood. They are archivists, researchers, art historians and art dealers, building managers, residents of two neighborhood buildings. The subject is Laukhuff's Bookstore, here from 1916-1960, a gathering place for cultural exchange—with vision and inspiration from the owner. It is here that poet Hart Crane met William Sommer one of this city's iconic painters. The relationship was important to both.

SUNDAY MORNING APPLES
To William Sommer

The leaves will fall again sometime and fill
The fleece of nature with those purposes
That are your rich and faithful strength of line.

> But now there are challenges to spring
> In that ripe nude with head
> > reared
>
> Into a realm of swords, her purple shadow
> Bursting on the winter of the world
> From whiteness that cries defiance to the snow.

A boy runs with a dog before the sun, straddling
Spontaneities that form their independent orbits,
Their own perennials of light
In the valley where you live
> (called Brandywine).

> I have seen the apples there that toss you secrets,—
> Beloved apples of seasonable madness
> That feed your inquiries with aerial wine.
> Put them again beside a pitcher with a knife,
> And poise them full and ready for explosion—
> The apples, Bill, the apples!   —*Hart Crane*

From: "The Collected Poems of Hart Crane" by Hart Crane, published by *Liveright Publishing Corp.*, New York. Copyright 1933, Liveright, Inc.

William Sommer's tribute to Hart Crane. The two met over wine and cheese at Laukhuff's Bookstore.

To William Sommer
Sunday Morning Apples
By Hart Crane

The leaves will fall again sometime and fill
The fleece of nature with those purposes
That are your rich and faithful strength of line.

But now there are challenges to spring
In that ripe nude with head
reared
Into a realm of swords, her purple shadow
Bursting on the winter of the world
From whiteness that cries defiance to the snow.

A boy runs with a dog before the sun, straddling
Spontaneities that form their independent orbits,
Their own perennials of light
In the valley where you live
(called Brandywine).

I have seen the apples there that toss you secrets,-
Beloved apples of seasonable madness
That feed your inquiries with aerial wine.
Put them again beside a pitcher with a knife.
And poise them full and ready for explosion-
The apples, Bill, the apples!

72   The Apples   Lent by Mr. and Mrs. Sol A. Bauer

William Sommer's tribute to Hart Crane. The two met over wine and cheese at Laukhuff's Bookstore.

Architects have mentored us with new experiences that enhance our grasp of special spaces; a renovated Severance Hall matching the quality of the music, The Temple an interior renovation making every former conformant proud of heritage and a future as a performing arts space, The Cleveland Trust bank building at 9th and Euclid given a future as a much needed grocery store to feed a growing downtown population. A new hotel, a masterful conversion of the Board of Education administration building has focused on the soul of the city. They have used local craftspersons, artisans and devoted project management that valued their work on behalf of the city.

Peter B. Lewis Building at Case Western Reserve University, designed by Frank Gehry.

Cover of *Cleveland Goes Modern*, Nina and Jim Gibans' joint project.

Observing, visiting working sessions, talking to leaders and artists we learn about risk, change, compatibility, and camaraderie. The stories about these realities sustain us. It isn't just architects, but the multi-disciplined teams of people that make the Playhouse Square complex alive — one that keeps improving an ever-evolving city. The vitality of the University Circle development is almost overwhelming. The neighborhoods led by musicians and music, theatre and dance venues, artists and galleries audiences and people sitting inside or on green spaces, on patios, and taking on new environments for living that have been developing these later years have allowed us to thrive on the spirit and community pride — it makes its way into everyone's "being".

Over sixty years the past lives in corners of our life every day; these developments look to the next generations. That is the design of our life.

It is not only the organizations that have nurtured us but the people espousing the same causes, who walked door to door, up and down streets, attended concerts and plays, gallery openings. **Better still on the days when we were the ONLY ones at artists' studios and galleries when we** could *really* see the artwork. In the same vein, Sunday afternoon chamber music concerts at a small church almost allowing us to *really* hear the sound of each instrument and almost read the musical pages with the artists. There are a cluster of us who see a corner of the world this way. We are eager to hear our favorites and to explore what might become a favorite.

From *Cleveland Goes Modern*. The major joint Gibans project other than raising a family. Our Mount Everest!

Ernst Payer House of the mid-50s in pristine condition. From the previous book, *Cleveland Goes Modern*.

Ernst Payer House of the mid-50s in pristine condition. From the previous book, Cleveland Goes Modern.

Jim worked with Don Hisaka, clearly one of Cleveland's most talented architects.

We are eager to learn. The Morgan Conservatory is a place we learn. Unique, it makes use of a mid-city warehouse – and creates a magnificent place for learning about paper, a far cry from the heavy printing industry of the 20th century housed in the Caxton Building, which provided livelihood for many artists. Understanding paper and complexities of papermaking possibilities links us all over the world and adds solid and exciting dimension to Cleveland's artistic growth.

The real question is how this appreciation, enthusiasm, ability to keep growing throughout life translates to the next generation? Schools and colleges, churches and almost every kind of organization are educational in all or part of their mission. One may try to do it formally through formal classes, workshops, bibliographies. We harvest ideas and impressions every minute of a day (even in our dreams). It is the ones that grow that are important. No matter how old we are. What are the sparks that will generate present and future involvement in this place? The "keepers", sources of inspiration, keep changing with new generations. We do not need the beer nights preceding or after performances, pre-show discussions, nightcaps. Just give us directing by Victoria Bussert, solos by Julie Andrejuski, David Giffels reading his works. And new works with groups like Blackbird. Memory holds the voices of poets James Kilgore and Barbara Angell. This is our place.

Reflecting on the writing of the first brochure while still at college for a fledgling organization Young Audiences in NYC in the 1950s, (now the Center for Arts-Inspired Learning) it is awesome to experience the development of that group whose mission is to become the wellspring for the next generation of art appreciators and doers. It has focused on underserved populations way before it was the "mantra" of some many organizations.

Judy Rawson — photograph of a printing press from Morgan Conservatory. From the Gibans Collection.

We are teaching and being taught. Our colleagues and students are from all over the world and right here. How important is this place as opposed to the next place they live. Will they ever have a sense of belonging? Or are they like migrating birds ready for flight; ready for nesting?

Pictured: Cleveland Public Theatre. Photo by: Steve Wagner

Wade Lagoon and the Cleveland Museum of Art, University Circle.

Gordon Square. Photograph courtesy of Gregory Wilson.

Robert Maschke Architects Office and Gallery in Gordon Square.

Playhouse Square. Photograph courtesy of Roger Mastroianni.

Waterloo Arts

Tremont Arts Festival.
Photograph courtesy the Tremont Arts Festival.

78th Street Studios during a Third Fridays Event.
Photograph courtesy of Gregory Wilson.

James A. Garfield Memorial at Lake View Cemetery.
Photography courtesy of Lake View Cemetery.

Chapter 3:
Education Ourselves and a Community

The Old Arcade, Cleveland Memory Project, Cleveland State University, Michael Schwartz Library Special Collections. Referred to by Jennifer Coleman in the "CityProwl Cleveland" podcast.

When Walter Benjamin wrote his massive journals: *ARCADES,* he used his indoor vantage point to observe people. A lifetime of note taking. Isn't that what we all do? Build a life based on how people act, respond, and create. That's it, most of the time. Its form varies. Our own solid grounding gave us a sense of place, identity and institutional memory. This is a treasure at a time when people move around and spend much of their lives adjusting to new environments. It is like continually coming in on the second act of a play. One of the enjoyable roles that seem important has been for us to help newcomers (whatever that means) connect to the past. Many times they have no priority for it, but they usually appreciate it in time. They were not in this place at some past time but are now. Community building takes time; because there is so much mobility, it is difficult to connect with "place" — that's part of the success of social media; it creates its own communities. They may or may not be physical places.

There may be many stories about building communities; the uniqueness of two stories that have created the Shaker Heights over the past decades is our center of gravity. They are the soul of this place.

- This generation has a hard time absorbing the story about saving the Shaker Lakes areas from becoming a freeway in the 1960s. The Shaker Lakes Nature Center, The Doan Brook Watershed Partnership, the present collective of citizens, businesses, non-profit organizations and local Northeast Ohio city governments continues a decades — old process of the stewardship and protection, restoration, of the urban watershed of the extension of the Lakes through the Brook down to Lake Erie. Saving parklands: fields, forests, marsh, lakes, stream and ravine has meant that this habitat for thousands of species of plants and wildlife, and birds has provided an environment vital for humane living. All because people cared. Our daughter, now an honored organic farmer in Oregon, did her senior project at the Shaker Lakes Nature Center. Lake Erie is the horizon line from our 11th floor apartment at Shaker Square, usually a thin gray-white outline — the shore that sits edging the forest of green, brown or white depending on the season.

Grey

    Grey   warming the neck of the city
                      covers like a grandmother's
        cowl
        shale
                roof of clouds, always hovering

    Grey

          This has always been so
          When glaciers melted into lakes
          and stopped at the lip
                history stirring grey upon grey
                into churning tides
                this deep caldron roiling
                turning and rolling
                angrier than giants
                bawdier than sailors
                high on waves.

          This is our sea
          Where lapping tongues
          drink into shorelines
          taste wetted beaches
          molasses dark sand
          where rocks anchor homes
          looking out to see
          through mist, another shore
          following the rugged rim
                    around an edge.

    Grey

    Grey   shading the eyes of the city
                  covers like thin blinds hanging
        straight
        shale
                roof of clouds, always hovering

Grey

        This is our sea
        Where grey mist settles on the surface
        and sun sometimes slices water
        like a diamond necklace
        Narcissi, the cities, see themselves
        in the images of iron stacks
        in bridges arching edge to edge
        cutting into sky and wind.
        Which was the wind
        "What is the wind, what is it?"

        This is the lake
        When clouds lay combed
        by a sunlit feathered canopy
        or layer thick encaustic covering
        the lake rolling and flapping over history
        folding into the shore
        blanketing our past and future.

Grey
Grey   warming the neck of the city
            covers like a grandmother's
    cowl
    shale
            roof of clouds, always hovering
Grey.

                                        —NFG

Excerpts published in "Great Lake Erie: Imagining an Inland Sea", SPACES, 2000.

Bad Water, 1991. Donald Harvey (American, 1941-). Photograph on aluminum; steel and rubber; overall: 188.7 x 214.1 x 6.9 cm (74 1/4 x 84 1/4 x 2 11/16 in.). The Cleveland Museum of Art, Gift of Mr. and Mrs. Richard A. Zellner 1998.118

Lori Kella *Blue Ore Boat*, 2013 Archival pigment print, 30" x 30"

Michael Loderstadt Installation view from exhibition: "Urban Evidence: Contemporary Artists Reveal Cleveland", 1996 Shown at Happy Dog event, September 2015.

- Our children were part of the efforts to integrate the Shaker Heights schools in the 1960s. The story of the multi-faceted and determined community project, a national model, still resonates in major broadcast productions and a library exhibition traveling through the Unites States now. Community meetings, decisions about which schools our children would attend, and putting our actions where our dedication to diversity lay dominated our lives during those days. Residents of our apartment building at Shaker Square include Carl Stokes, first black Mayor of Cleveland, Zelma George, United States Ambassador to the United Nations and the Director of Fair Housing who can tell the story of the breakthrough in financing minority housing at a time when there was outright residential discrimination. It is a small "neighborhood" within a neighborhood, housing family friends from childhood, colleagues from elementary school and college days, and old neighbors from our home. One resident was born in the same hospital as I during the same month.

The lasting influence of these community-wide efforts is monumental. Grasping their meaning is difficult for today's generations. Participation is soul satisfying.

The civic energy behind these projects and their implementation was not about money. It was about beliefs, stamina, and values of citizens who prevailed. Other important stories are buried in the replies to the surveys—the Metropolitan Parks, Lakeview Cemetery, University Circle institutions — histories that relied on visionary civic leaders whose individual clout established memorable legacies over the years. The efforts reflect vision, passion, influence and money. No one would deny their significance; their genesis and survival *feels* different. The places: buildings, galleries, foundations, named for them are all over the city. Today, in addition, there are newer names and newer money establishing important legacies for the future.

Soul is about how one "feels about something, not about what one does". Allen C. Ford, a member of the Cozad-Ford families, perhaps the only living storyteller about those monumental days still mentors young and old, informally tutoring leaders, institutions, making sure that the legacies of Cleveland are preserved. His influence in the preservation of the East Cleveland Township Cemetery and the monumental Lake View Cemetery is palpable in any discussions.

When we came back to Cleveland, it all started with an examination of creativity, taping the conversation and logging the process for a multi-media event in the late 60s. Daniel Hodermarsky, head of the Supplementary Education Center of the Cleveland Public Schools, Don Erb, stretching musical concepts as composer at the Cleveland Institute of Music and Larry Berger, TRI-C Dancer/choreographer working through ideas and concept. I wanted to know about the creative process—when is a work done; or is it ever.

We teach ourselves every day. We are never too old to begin a new thought, make a new friend. Today it was how to deal with, learn about using a motorized wheelchair, a smart phone, keep one foot right in front of the other...always something new.

Digging into histories through creating film: *Potter and Mellen: Transcending Time; Shaker Square Video (with WOIO); University Circle: Creating a Sense of Place; Pepper Ridge Rd. The vision of Robert Little;* and *Creative Essence; Cleveland's Sense of Place,* I met Cleveland head-on.

Every day we are surrounded by events and experiences that invite participation. How we engage, take up the challenge, use our time, deploy our energy, gather momentum and take risks that have potential takes self-confidence and attitude.

Beginning many years ago, using whatever possible means, that confidence grew by finding something worth writing about, positive actions to take, persons to encourage,

Every day. The community is an educator. The world around us has become so bizarre that the sense of place, identity and institutional memory are stabilizers and points from which to start looking around us.

About 100 years ago, 1916-1967 there was the bookstore Laukhuff's where two souls of Cleveland met. The friendship of William Sommer, (1867-1949) whose mural of early Cleveland is seen as one enters the Brett Reading Room of the Cleveland Public Library, and Hart Crane (1899-1932), poet, whose examination of bridges started in Cleveland well before he wrote *The Bridge,* became closest of friends. Sommer, for twenty-two years one of Otis Lithography Company's most prolific poster artists, joined up with Crane for meals, music and discussion. From John Unterecker's biography of Crane, *Voyager.* "If Crane can be said to have a 'teacher,' Sommer was that teacher. Sommer acted as surrogate father, counselor, drinking companion, confidant infallible conversationalist. In Sommer, Hart found an equal, a man of genius whom he could talk to with absolute ease."

Daniel Thompson (Poet Laureate of Cuyahoga County) and I met on Hart Crane's birthday in the parking lot of the Heart Association Building at 115th St across the street from where Crane lived, to read and celebrate. Then we would go the old Euclid Tavern (now the Happy Dog-Euclid Tavern) to read our own poetry.

Daniel devoted himself to those in the jails—carried a walkie-talkie to connect with anyone who needed him. When he died in 2005, West 2nd street was named Daniel's Way in his memory. It was the least we could do for an honored poet.

Daniel Thompson and Richard Howard. Friends with varying personalities and points of view.

I "found"/heard this poem at our yearly potluck celebration of Daniel at Horseshoe Lake in 2015. It had won first prize at the annual Hessler Street Fair.

for the godfather, daniel thompson (1935-2004)

at the outpost coffee house you said, "you seem like a nice kid,
    now go away"
at the "together help line" it was, "hey kid, don't i know you?"
after a reading of some hot-off-the-press buddhist third class
    junkmail oracle jazz ,
you advised, "try to stay out of jail" then offered your card, "just
    in case"

years later, down in kent, you got right in my face,
and said, "nice work, ever read at a junk yard?"

poet laureate, king of hearts, jack of the arts

tradesman, fisherman, great grey chief

bondsman, bread man, blanket man, thief

stealing time, and offering rhyme in return, you backed me into
    gigs:
"can you pick me up?" "got a minute?"
"what are you doin' right now?"
"any poems on you?"

so we did militant larynx, midnight poets, at the arabica, hart
    crane's valentine,
and readings in honor of d.a. levy and langston hughes,
PAND at cain park, dan's slam, luigi's in your ear, mark's reader,
barry's library, suzanne's book store,
on stage at CPT, hessler street fair, barking spider,
and gigs with sparks, salinger, melton, drumplay and brother
    ray

so when they say, "did you know him well?"
i say, "hell, every poet did"

and every one of the hundreds who actually went to church
    that day
had something to say, a poem to read, a story to tell

so, with a kiss of the ring and a wave of the hand,
i say thank you to the best damn poet in the land
of cleve,
from which, so many artist's eventually split

but not you, daniel,
you stayed, and the band played,
and we all got paid
in smiles,
and miles of poems,
good deeds,
words to heed

and we still hear you in the wind
as it whips across the flats, cuts carefully up superior,
takes one-o-five to east boulevard, then jogs to juniper
whispers across the mic at the spider,
and playfully rustles leaves and tussles hair,
at the annual hessler street fair

                                                    Jeffrey Bowen

Mentors in formal settings—schools gave me structure (Latin at Laurel School (Miss Stoner)); Jewish Education at Fairmount Temple (Libbie Braverman); Cleveland Museum of Art (Sherman Lee). These were not debaters; they were mandators. I thrived in unstructured settings when I was ready to take on responsibility for my own learning. That meant learning to live with disability, risk, challenge — within multi-disciplines and informal structures—characteristics of classes, workshops, projects I have taken hold of and implemented in schools, colleges, galleries, arcades, coffee shops, libraries, created venues and streets. They are all learning places. People teach us all of the time. Unexpectedly and intentionally.

Thoughts on Being Away by January
A Letter to Certain Friends
From Richard Howard
Christmas 1954

LEAVING in the dead season, before
Any lovely beginning, even
Before the furtive movements of ice
Melting and the drain of dirty snow ——
Leaving is so easy in a month
Like this, when the merest bird marking
The sky is bound to be unclean, and
Whatever steps we take remind us
How far down in the ground the cold goes.
      Villon, shivering in black Paris,
Said he forgot the sun, wrote about
Wolves in the streets and watched the ink freeze
In its pot, prayed for fire and his life.

After six seasons of turnabout
Weather in the air I've known since the first
I knew there was air at all ——a fter
Six equal variation of cloud
And clearing — I think of Villon now
And tell myself: no one leaves behind
The real winter. Cold follows within ——
Even when we wriggle to the warm
Pains of April, who can abandon
The weight and wan consequence of frost
Beside himself, the inner weather?
Not to run away then, but to face
Up better to a freshening wine
That comes from foreign parts, I would quit
Our dark town and in it both my loves
And labors. Detached? Of course not, but
Determined to gather somewhere else
The dust we all shall eat —— pounds, they say,
Before coming clean.

                        Leaving, though, means
Losing as well, and loss, at least so
Far as I have learned, is somewhat less
Only when remarked: therefore, this grey
Christmastime, I think that I shall think
Gratefully upon the eighteen months
Weathered with you or withered, so bright
Some of them and some of them so bare ——
Burning time and bald, balanced alike
In a granted or a grudging scale,
Time, and all of it (broken and whole)
That must be brought, as Villon said,
With me where I go.
As I go now.

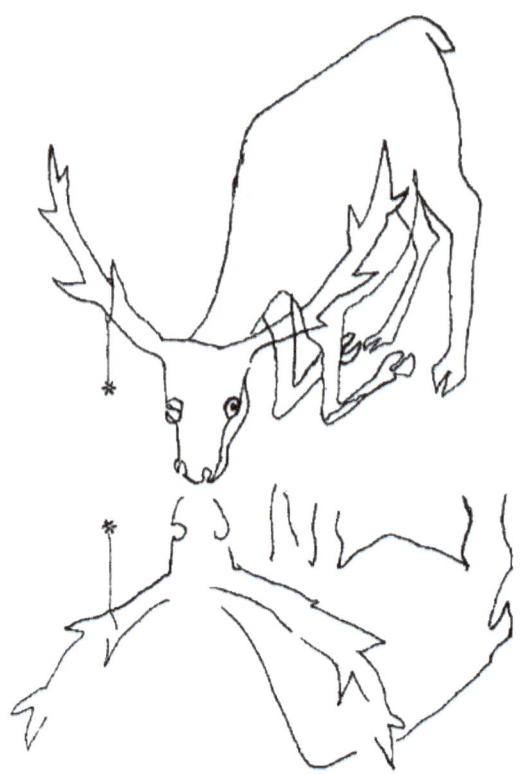

Chapter 4:
Greening Our Spirit

Photography of Shaker Lakes from "Preserving Our Natural Heritage", *Shaker Life*, Feb/Mar 2012, by Caydie Heller. Photograph courtesy of *Shaker Life*.

Green sustains us perhaps more than any other color. Grasses cushioning our steps, meadows nurturing burgeoning crops, clusters of trees defining vision or framing our worlds as we move and they move – those experiences help us through any day. We may not even notice as we rush through our lives. It was engineers planning to remove lakes, displacing grass with concrete, surrounding a verdant community with the noise and environment of a highway that motivated the citizens of Shaker Heights to come together around such environmental change. A mirror of our lives, the Shaker Lakes-Doan Brook story is perhaps the most important one reminding us how different the scene from our window might be if it were not that our forefathers and mothers — really the recent generation — cared about the soul of our environment. As big as this story was, there are many people who use the bike paths, walk around the lakes, *feel* affection for the area who do not know how fortunate they are. Others know every crack in the walk; turn in the lake's edge, and every bend in the curb.

Dahlias, a specialty of the Doll and Gibans families.
Photography courtesy of Henry Doll.

Dahlias, a specialty of the Doll and Gibans families.
Photography courtesy of Henry Doll.

Gentleman farmer Henry Doll, friend and neighbor growing dahlias and sunflowers, zucchinis and beets delivers them by bike. Shares jams and sauces stirred on his stove, and pies for every taste. Right from his back yard on Van Aken Boulevard, a main thoroughfare. A long appreciation of his flowers started at the restaurant FIRE when he brought his dahlias to our daughter Beth's engagement party there. He has visited Beth's organic farm, Backyard Gardens in Joseph, Oregon. Her life's work began at the Shaker Lakes Nature center where she interned. The North Union Farmer's Market on Shaker Square, now two decades old, entices thousands of folks each Saturday offering fresh meats, breads, lettuces, mushrooms, eggs, and conversation. By one o'clock emptied vans disappear and the green becomes a spot for sitting or listening or eating — an outdoor living — dining room.

The development of the North Union Farmer's Market has changed the patterns of growing, buying, living and eating all over the city. Cleveland has bought into healthy living backed by hospitals that promote healthy eating. It is the weekly mecca for congeniality, procurement, and satisfaction. Growers put things aside, bring what is popular and fill large orders with just the right apples or the special pastries only available there. Restaurant Chefs –such as Zach Bruell pick up their fresh produce. People schedule their work lives, daytime social lives so they can get there early enough to get the food they plan for and get on with the day. There are no parking places after 9am. We can walk.

The word has spread throughout the neighborhoods as if community and backyard gardening is a really good thing – seems similar to close-in family farms where we bought corn when we were children. This generation of gardeners dream of owning food trucks to help generate revenue. In a flatland city on a Lake, green land is precious. We do not have the rolling hills of other areas of the country. In Northeast Ohio with a history of heavy industry, planning green land has been particularly valuable. With foresight, the John D. Rockefellers and Jeptha Wades and the leaders of that special time at the end of the 1800s and beginning of the 20th century saw to it that this city developed parks like Rockefeller Park, Wade Park and the Metropolitan Park system. These interests were satisfying the need to create an environment commensurate with the industrial growth.

Countryside Conservancy was established in 1999 as a private nonprofit dedicated to assisting Cuyahoga Valley National Park to preserve the fading rural character of the Cuyahoga Valley. Its innovative land use program rehabilitates farms and farmland within the park and leases these farmsteads to be farmed and cared for by independent family farmers. Today, there are 11 working farms committed to sustainable agriculture who participate in weekly year around farmers markets in the national park.

North Union Farmers Market at Shaker Square, taken on their twentieth anniversary celebration, July 18, 2015. Photograph courtesy of Lauren Clifford Photography. Weekly visit with thousands of other friends to the North Union Farmer's Market.

Rockefeller Park Bridge, designed by Charles Schweinfurth. Photograph courtesy of the Library of Congress, HABS OHIO, 18-CLEV, 16—2.

We were part of a bigger mind-set as well. During the time of the industrial revolution, the Cuyahoga Valley had suffered from pollution, and overall lack of maintenance. In the early 1900's the idea of protecting beautiful land across the United States was taking hold (The National Park Service is 100 years old). The Cuyahoga Valley was one area that came to their attention and seemed the perfect place to establish a National Park. It is located along the **Cuyahoga River** between **Akron** and **Cleveland** and is the only national park in Ohio. It was established in 1974 as the **Cuyahoga Valley National Recreation Area** and was designated as a national park in 2000.

Theses green areas, full of urban plantings or wildflowers, all kinds of native birds and animals are important to the soul of Cleveland.

We have participated in planning sessions and cheered the development of the Ohio & Erie Canal

Towpath trail developed by the National Park Service, the major trail through Cuyahoga Valley National Park. Family trips on the **Cuyahoga Valley Scenic Railroad** have allowed our grandchildren an important peak into area history as they traveled along the towpath from Rockside Road to Akron, getting off/on at any of the 6 other stops along the way or walked along the same path that the mules used to tow the canal boats loaded with goods and passengers.

The Towpath Trail follows the historic route of the **Ohio & Erie Canal**. Before the canal was built, Ohio was a sparsely settled wilderness where travel was difficult and getting crops to market was nearly impossible. The canal, built between 1825 and 1832, provided a successful transportation route from **Cleveland**, on **Lake Erie**, to **Portsmouth**, on the **Ohio River**. The canal opened up Ohio to the rest of the settled eastern United States.

We have treasured the Soul of Downtown: The Eastman Garden an outdoor sitting room next to the Cleveland Public Library — a special green place. Quiet lunch hours, purposeful walkthroughs, a sunlift on a grey day, next to the hub of information, exhibition, discussion, debate and the underpinning for exhibitions such "Charles F. Scweinfurth, Uncompromising Architect of Cleveland's Valiant Age".

Laila Voss, *A Chaotic Symphony: The Catch-All Net*, 1996

Cleveland's Metroparks, and the Cuyahoga Valley National Park –the "emerald necklaces", and the Ohio and Erie Canal Towpath Trail– the flourishing bookend capturing the brilliance and soul of northeast Ohio's green lands, waterways, bikeways and "esprit de corps"—the dance in the grass, the walk in the woods, the birding and animal seeking, tossing stones in the ever-widening circles of water in quiet puddles or running streams. Treats for sunny days.

Community gardens

We always had a garden. A cherry tree honored my 11th birthday; Jim's father and he grew roses. My love of the reddest ones that came in from his garden on the second floor roof of the garage in our condominium was my summer highlight – a celebration of us. From the 11th floor we could look over a forest of trees to the Lake, had close neighbors who were farmers, a farmer's market down the street and roses on the table. Our daughter is an honored organic farmer who owns Backyard Gardens in Joseph Oregon – complete with CSAs, Farmers' market, catering from there to St. Croix and has been our teacher about healthy eating and naturopathy. Her interests started here at the Food Bank and the Shaker Lakes Nature Center and then in Costa Rica, The Land Institute in Kansas, and The Center for Agroecology and Sustainable Food Systems in Santa Cruz, California. There she was immersed in the teaching and research around ecological sustainability and social justice.

The red roses, chives, daffodils define Jim's garden at Shaker Towers where we lived. He gardens as therapy, and digs for camaraderie and solace, which resonates with both of us. His first garden 30 years ago replaced that of Dorothy Fuldheim who lived here, and had her red hair done in the beauty parlor here, preparing for her iconic broadcast over Channel 5, known by everyone of that era. *Eighteen Gardens and their Gardeners,* a poetry and photography publication, gathered the stories from gardeners who came from Cleveland's inner city, Romania, and from homes nearby where former homes and gardens meant a lot to them. Transplanted statuettes, a fishpond and bulbs resonated their past lives when they moved here because of the green rooftop.

Cool Color White

Roses, tiger lilies, silver dollars
as fresh as manuscripts, tapestries, paintings
history a catalogue of plantings
for ordering.
There is my canvas—
on the roadsides, along buildings,
traveling in woods and backyards,

the crevices of trees and holes—
my window, my gate, my wall;
I am a painter in this space.

Medallions on old gates, flower forms,
tapestries guide me to gardens of castles and meadows
hand-making history;
I stand up to history.
How much is in this garden?
How have I invented with my eye?
How many years of yellow in a marigold?
What day did the spring-blue turn to summer-azure?
Where did this dahlia get a pink perfect for today?
Daffodils by mid-afternoon
singing yellow on my wallpaper.
I know the people and the moods, the position of the sun
and shadows.
Time is in a garden, a life span of color—
delirious eye.
This rose is mine;
How many years it edged a wall and saw the sun,
its folds close in on the warmth of a moment?
I look into a lily
and drink it's cool-white color
like O'Keefe and water.
My Flemish fields are fresh
I pick bouquets with my eyes
These are my fields; spring shoots
early green and color.

Where do gardens begin to be remembered?
Purple vines on the city walls,
orange on southern trees,
clipped around poles, trees, intersects,
trimmed city parlor.
I write home about other things
but remember gardens

and when they came into my home.
My table is a Dutch still life,
lily for lily, crisp color in a vase.

Picasso and Matisse paint my bouquets
I am a gardener.
I plant whatever I can
whenever I want.
I remember especially pink and purple
cascading on century-old walls.
(Was it like that in Babylon?)
I add red from roses.

—NFG

from *Eighteen Gardens and their Gardeners*, Ohio Arts Council Artists project, 1999, Nina Freedlander Gibans

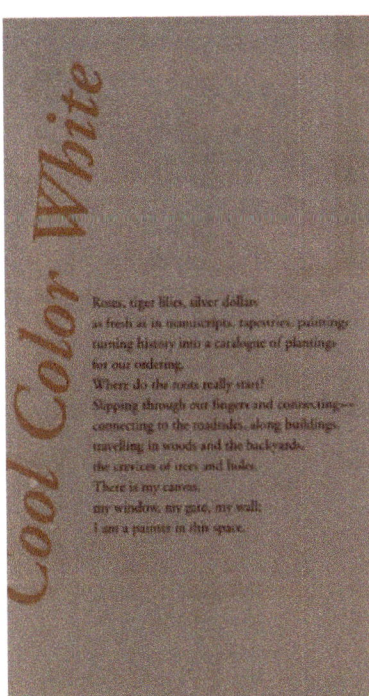

"Cool Color White" by Nina Gibans. This poem was inspired by a trip to Barcelona, Spain and the gardens at Shaker Towers.

Jim and Gardens

Roses from my father
Herbs I can eat
Color for every room
Dig away worries
I cut flowers and share perennials
I take pride
Getting to know people
The sun is warm ideas grow
Tales are wrapped in the cutting shears
This moment belongs to us.

—NFG

I never wanted to go this way
never in Spring when the bulbs come up
and surprise me from last Fall
I check out the buds
And design my travel route for beauty
The neighborhood awakens
With the growers, and the gatherers'
Stories.

—NFG

Gardening is in our DNA. Photograph by Michael Loderstedt

Chapter 5:
Cornerstones: Physical and Spiritual

The cornerstones — the physical city and the spiritual city intertwine in the built spaces that call us together for all events for communality, discussion, entertainment. The mix of the dozens of ethnic groups—we are all ethnic at some point of heritage—mine was Lithuanian but the hard-core Lithuanians here wanted lineage that they approved. The churches sang gospels and chorales in communal voice and native tongues; the Bohemian halls echoed with the accordions and polkas, the colorful festivals have adorned our neighborhoods with colorful costumes. My perspective is positioned by having been in many buildings, a painted wall project throughout several neighborhoods, the work of commissioned artists of all views and hues in the community in the 70s, wall murals by invited artists on "dirty" walls, and being there — to celebrate, play the trumpet, dance the jig, read the poems, sing-a-long. These artists and those through the years have left their mark in publications, in recordings, in our hearts and on our walls. We have watched them produce and teach us all from their color of their subject matter, styles, voices, and media.

But the bridges, the Arcade, and Severance Hall and most recently the Cleveland Museum of Art are special physical gems. On our anniversaries, we have commissioned sculptors, weavers, photographers, painters and on our 60th, Amy Casey, currently the artist of the 2016 Cleveland Public Library card artist's series wove the Arcade, Lakeview Terrace, Severance Hall and the Cleveland Museum of Art into our small commissioned print.

When people ask what your favorite building is, Jim answers, without hesitation, "Severance Hall!" Why? It's actually a rather strange building because of its varied styles within one complex. But that's also what makes it so fascinating. As was very popular at the time, there's Egyptian, there's Art Deco, there's Art Moderne – All of these things are sort of wrapped up in this building, each in their own space.

My memories include concerts my parents brought me to hear, school concert trips and a need to plumb the archives for various projects. The sound has never not been beautiful—one of the week's highpoints always. Listening again on Sunday afternoons radio, over 80 years on our Telefunken and changing listening systems gave additional meaning to this space. I was there again as the space emblazoned the music.

I feel that way now about the Mixon Recital Hall at the Cleveland Institute of Music. Sublime and perfect for smaller ensembles.

It's what happens inside these spaces and to us as we encounter them that resonates.

Almost a Find

When I found Hart Crane's high school picture
in a classroom-made museum by today's
children digging their past.

I asked him what he was doing there.
"poems" he said and we went to see bridges.

When I talked to Russell (Atkins)
at the library where he met Langston Hughes
we celebrated.
in the basement
and sat in the very seats.

When d.a.levy died
We cried.
When the day exceeds its bounds
of nonsequitur
he makes sense.
And we celebrate
These are our poets
The world has only borrowed them
For one good read.

—NFG

The Bridges That Hart Crane Left[1]
dedicated to Alberta Turner
"city forms (are) more beautiful because they were never meant to be beautiful...."[2]

Born in the moonlight, this would be home.
Bonfires, beach-brush, clearings for homesteads
a chrysalis for hand crafting
and making a city.
The moon hung onto this place
and blessed it with half eye on water
river calming lake waves after the bend.

Portage from canal to canal criss-crossing distances
carrying dreams over trails. Paths became streets
Euclid, Woodland to Lake Erie. A small plaque speaks:
"The meeting of the Portage Trail and the Buffalo Trail."[3]
"HERE, hear!"
Not easy on the Cuyahoga

       strangers and natives
              barter for corn, barter
            first neighborhoods

These are the bridges Hart Crane left
these shapes a museum of forms
piercing skies black on grey or blue
some slight movement, a slight sideways shift (or is it the wind?),

---

[1] Poem published in "And So I Must Imagine", Nina Freedlander Gibans, Xlibris 2010
[2] *Margaret Bourke White, photographer, (1904-1971) Discussions between Hart Crane (1899-1932) and Bill Sommer on painters SEEING in color and poets HEARING in words from the* <u>Transformations</u> *exhibition catalogue, Cleveland Museum of Art, 1996*
[3] Sign at 107th and Euclid Avenue about Indian paths.

some levered up and down,
some untouchable — invisible cases preserving them
too heavy to move; saved by imagined energy
of the truckloads of heavy raw materials.

Cover of And So I Must Imagine, 2009, a book of poems by Nina Gibans. Launching of the book in October 2010 at the City Steak House in Wooster, OH, the site of the original Freedlander Department Store (1868)

Drawings of these bridges were commissioned by the Cleveland Children's Museum to accompany the brochure for their Bridges exhibit. Drawings by Carol McMenamin

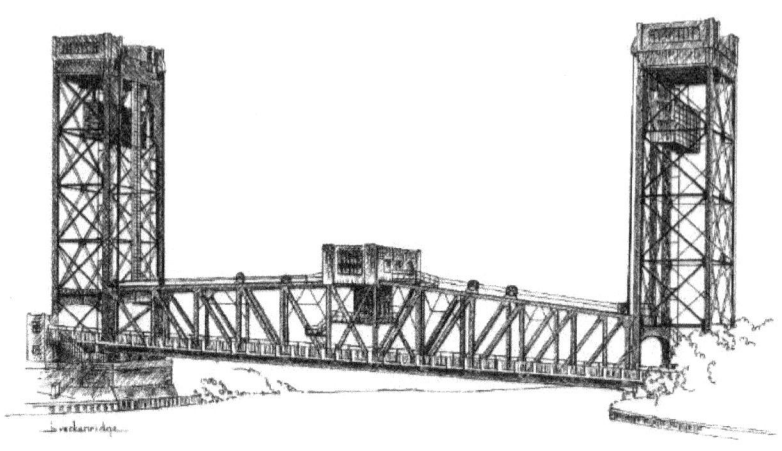

Columbus Road Lift Bridge

1836-1940   Columbus Road Lift Bridge

1836: The only covered bridge in Cleveland, it had a small moveable section. 1870: a county bridge. 1895: double swing bridge (a first of its kind). 1940: a WPA project as part of river widening project. Site of the "Bridge War" of 1837, when Ohio City merchants did not want this short cut to downtown to disturb their vision of a "world trade center" on the Ox Bow to the north.

History gathered from the silt, soil, stones, water —
buildup of rock salt bedrock eroding, melting, burying truth and secrets uncovering,
picking apart our being?
Was it centuries ago or yesterday or now that we bury the story?
Was it always a guess?

Artisans from Europe; craftsmen from Ohio dig
for Hanna, Corning, Mather, Holden,
a smokestack, a railroad for each,
a park for Rockefeller. Foundations and gardens of memory
for those who came here to plant their history.

Frames and fenestration down the halls of streets
stop for a turret, a doorway,
a doorway, a pleasing arch,
balancing brick or stone or wood
images crossing oceans of ideas.
Hand painted wallpaper, living rooms and cornices, whorled wooded banisters,
history tumbles down staircases into the gardens.

      Workers gather tools
cut the earth, dig foundations
    raise walls for foundries
    and stoke the fires.

Detroit Street Bridge

1853   Detroit Street Bridge
Built by the Cleveland and Mahoning Railroad to reach the docks on the Cuyahoga River. Operated by the Erie Railroad until bankruptcy and abandoning the right of way. Two-barrel masonry 55 feet long, 93 feet wide, the oldest remaining bridge constructed of Berea sandstone with double skewed stone arches.

"City forms are beautiful because they were never meant for beauty."
Boat horns and whistles, the song of this city
bridges strong as bedrock
mills gorging tree sites keep blooming and dying
with the work seasons. Alleluia!

Smokestacks sang work songs,
trees were there before the stacks;
green, then gray and brown-dung sadness
Lamentations.

Wondering what we know for sure: hammer and chisel, worker and workload.
How long were days, how many breaks, whose humor got workers through a day,
what were the tragedies, the "faulted" estimates, the satisfactions?
Assembling history, piling up shapes from windows of airplanes,
poking up like stovepipes from earth to heaven
fast-moving cars, trucks running over noisy road grids,
thoughts from slow uneven walks over uneven pavement,
views of the long approach through a rearview mirror.

One worker slipped dockside
one never came home
footprints where they fell
anchoring the new city.

Superior Street Viaduct

1878 Superior Street Viaduct

86 feet above the river, replaced by the Detroit-Superior Bridge, first high-level bridge intended to heal the wounds of the Annexation of Ohio City in 1850. Sought to join east and west sides of Cleveland into a more integrated community. The westerly approach consisted of 8 arches; the easterly approach was of steel construction because the Cleveland, Columbus, Cincinnati and St. Louis railroad trackage precluded shore arches. Replaced because of accidents that might result because of the "draw" being open for boats.

In the thigh of the road beneath the stubble of stones
that lined the edge, beneath the brick top surface,
lies a history. Storekeepers sweep the top;
dirt slides through to the past.

Six solid city streets packed
with stores and homes, one gas station.
Baking and eating, families keep secret recipes
fresh for next generations.

    Sorrows and laughter
    woven into shawls
    covering shoulders
    at the cemetery.

Center Street Bridge

1901 *Center Street Swing Bridge.*

The only remaining swing bridge marks the site of the first downtown crossing east-west after the "Bridge War." It was completed one night by moonlight.

Coaxing boats underneath
coursing trips to the mills
playing games, or duty-bound
counting cars, waiting, holding time in the motorshed

people get out to look
and gossip the line to cross west or east
telling the same stories — the battles for the bridges,
people on the west side wanting to cross for food at the open market;
people on the east side coming home from shopping
on the west side bringing market apples in spring and fall
and east-side juicy rosy cheeked peaches for summer pies.
Cars line up unevenly like a towpath on the river bank,
Look at the tan and blue water metallic in the sun.

    Waves kneading the land
    like fresh dough
families spread onto the new
east and west.

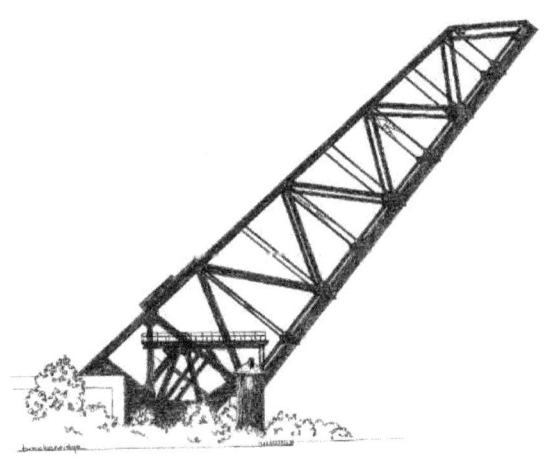

Baltimore and Ohio Railroad Bridge

Baltimore and Ohio Railroad Bridge

1907 Baltimore and Ohio Railroad Bridge #464 — Cleveland Valley and Recreational Bridge Swing Bridge

Blocked the channel to old river docks, the longest single track Scherzer bridge ever built. Is opened by rolling on a counterweight consisting of a toothed track. The motor on the bridge drives the rack and pinion to operate the bridge.

Stonecutters cut stone into pylons into sculpture again
putting their hands on the city
painters look at bridges from factory windows
from the shoreline, from lazy boats lying low
from the gull perch on the edge of broken boat wood stick
from the shallow sand beach, from the thin road down, from the high-rise.
How do bridges look now crowded with laughter and task?

Paintings call me to the river, 1833, 1934
where the sun shifts gears in an afternoon,
greenlands turn to reds and bronze, smoke and grey
I travel with the painter to his mural in the reading hall
where the city rises from the riverbed
a stone's throw from the river's eye.

    We made automobiles
        gas, electric and steam
        engines disappear into a fog
    of newer dreams.

Detroit-Superior High Level Viaduct

1918 *Detroit-Superior High Level Viaduct*

98 feet above the water, steel center span of nickel steel, it was the first high-level bridge to span the Cuyahoga without a "draw" or movable section for river traffic. By 1918 tall masts on sailing vessels were obsolete, making higher clearance openings unnecessary. 12 concrete arches with 2 levels: one for vehicles, and 2 sets of tracks for streetcars.

Every city section has a silent past. In one,
factory workers walked to work; ten minutes.
Home for lunch at the whistle.
Now no whistle; it's ten miles by car.
Street cleaners swap stories
languages mix and languish as cultures come and go
They are hungry for themselves.

Empty streetscapes stalk the city
one shopkeeper sweeps
as the day works its way across the shop-front
scattering debris like morning news
the loud voices in the wind, processions
for weddings and funerals, encrusted rumors,
sidewalk stories swept to the curb
roll into dust.

A paper moves along the street
lifted by uneven bursts of wind
and deserted thoughts. Between buildings,
split stones mirror sun
spot-colors on the city canvas.
Tarp and rags cover stains
An armchair on the curb collects history.

> White noise, 18-wheelers
> birds cling to the old
>   branches
> children shoot basketballs
>
> into the torn nets of their
>
>   lives.

Nickel Plate Railroad Viaduct

Several moveable bridges, a Trunnion Bascule Bridge (1920), Rolling lift bascule, railroad Lift Bridge (Nickel Plate Railroad Viaduct (1904, 1944, 1960) built over the older bridge so as not to delay traffic.

Water life and sounds of sunsets
lure birds gauging tides and movement
being carried along, or flying into color, beaks down, or wings on loft
positioned to prevail, hailing clouds, flaunting winds, the sun a chandelier.
Foraging history, fish and fishermen translate traditions and tough waters,
digging the past, scraping bottoms and surfaces for sustenance.

Lead smelters, paint   companies
    too many workers

    watch the city crumble

    into industry's dust.

Cleveland, Columbus, Cincinnati and St. Louis Railroad Bridge

Cleveland, Columbus, Cincinnati and St. Louis Railroad Bridge

1953 Cleveland, Columbus, Cincinnati and St. Louis (Big Four) Single Track

Railroad Bridge #4 received an American Institute of Steel Construction award as the "most beautiful steel bridge in Class IV."

Time lies in the crook of the river
ore boats struggle around new water craft
seeking lanes for working tugs
blocked by boaters seeking fun
or napping lightly.

Dance of the city; stop lights sway
spitfire voices blurred by passing cars
coming to composure in store windows.
sidewalks clearing
monochromatic high-rises
step into their shadows
grays, red-browns, burgundies
etched windows frame city sensors.

Night light celebrations
scattered homes spotted through the trees
birdsongs calm nerves;
Porch a rocking swing moving in the wind.
rhythms in wood. Alleyways of brick
dappled from hoof marks; this year's running path.

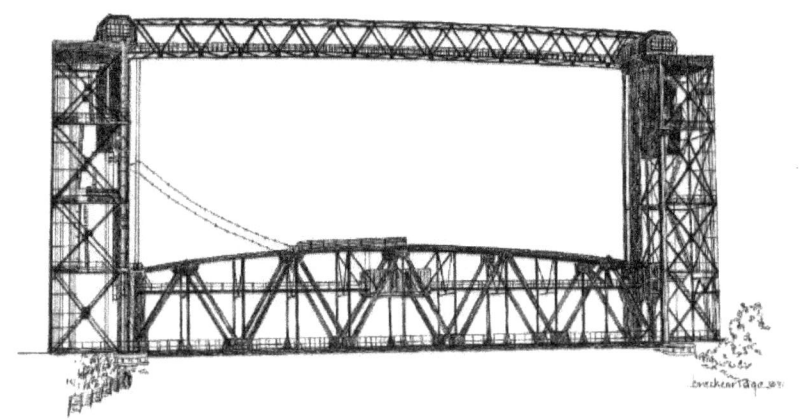

Conrail Bridge

1976 Conrail Bridge #1

Double track lift bridge, 265 feet, 98-250 feet clear opening motors in the bridge structure operate cables that raise and lower the span. Works like an elevator. Operator in tower on west bank controls trains from Berea to Collinwood by a track block system for safe operation. It's on the main line of Conrail between New York and Chicago—2nd busiest carrying heavy freight through Cleveland.

Around the bend the lake-grey distance
waves glower, walloping beaches
pushing the shoreline, pounding like heartbeats
Around the bend the lake-grey distance
waves glower, walloping beaches
pushing the shoreline, pounding like heartbeats
crashing into rock , falling into itself
grey heaps rise and flatten,
exhausted.

Shoreline rumble

trains and boats discuss
the world beyond
the ore boat and craft debate.

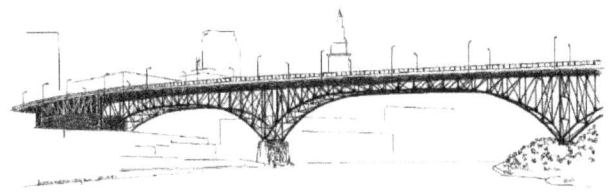

Main Avenue Bridge

These are the bridges that Hart Crane left
invisible cases preserving them
as the sun spotlights tufts of green
silent pickings in the brown fields
from the attics of the city, letters sucked with leaves
caught in grates, love tossed out to tree lawns
collecting life's odd belongings and potential.
Work songs and lamentations.
lighted shapes

    celebrate form

    against the night sky.

—NFG

Hart Crane Memorial Park under the Columbus Road Bridge.

    I had crossed the swing bridges weekly over the Cuyahoga as a small child and owned them as we replicated their engineering innovation at the Children's Museum, identifying them with bronze labels. The Museum brought the sounds from the bridges out to the museum by telephone cable, by placing microphones on the bridges to capture the horns and river cacophony. Museum visitors could manipulate the sounds.

    I had coffee at the old Flat Iron pub with teachers, many times finding out about the bridges first hand. We sat at the blue sculpture honoring Hart Crane the poet by artist Gene Kangas at the Hart Crane Memorial Park (Columbus/Merwin Aves). Hart Crane helped me understand them.

We had gotten to know Bill Sommer (1867-1949) the painter when we followed him from wonderful gentle and colorful portraits, landscapes where one wanted to move with the line, and the mural of downtown Cleveland in the Brett Reading Room of the Cleveland Public Library. We spend weekends at Brandywine, where he had his country studio and was in his prime, holding forth with gatherings of students and friends continuing their in-town discussions of art, music and literature.

Interstate 90 Inner Belt Bridge

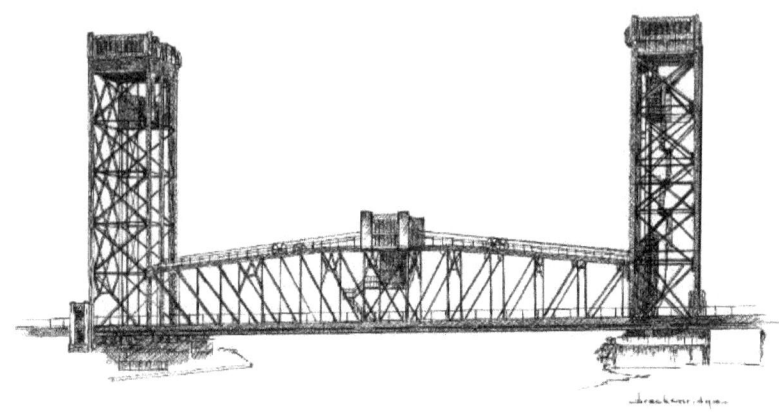

Carter Road Bridge

They sing to us; Sommer was Crane's soul mate — surrogate father, counselor, drinking companion, confidant, infallible conversationalist. In Sommer, Hart Crane found an equal, a man of genius, with whom he could discuss anything. [Sue Hanson, Hart Crane a Drawing by William Sommer, essay, Akron Northern Ohio Bibliophilic Society 1988]. Sommer left the bridges to Crane whose "room in Cleveland …was the center and beginning of all that I am and will ever be." They met there at 1709 E 115th St after work as well. As today's poets celebrated Crane's birthday across the street in the parking lot of the Heart Association mansion, we acknowledged the place, the poet and the first stages of *The Bridge,* his major work. [Hart Crane in Akron and Cleveland 1919-1923; Ohio Roads and the Bridges to *The Bridge,* ms by Olivier Alexis, 2007]

So I got to know the bridges in different ways over a lifetime.

William Sommer, *Portrait of Hart Crane*, c.1922. Matchstick on paper, 21 3/8" x 18 ¾". Kelvin Smith Library Special Collections & Archives, Case Western University.

A Conversation

Hart Crane, poet and Bill Sommer, painter meet at the bookstore; they hung out at Sommer's farm at Brandywine.

I.
Bridges soar with song
Hart Crane told Bill Sommer at the bookstore
"it's rock salt base beneath the riverbed, mountain high, arched and scooped."
Smokestacks are chords
the songs we sing
celebrate cocoons of smoke.

II.
The color of the country is never far away
when the sun shifts in an afternoon
green lands turn to reds and bronze
with sprays of meadow white and gold

I travel with the painter
fifteen miles east of the riverbed
ten miles south or to the west
a stone's throw from the painter eye
standing in the grasses picking color for my song.
Hallelujah!

III.
Coaxing us, Bill said he could *see* in color
To sing along; to sing again as he has sung.
I know I hear his words in color.
Amen.

—NFG

Charles F. Schweinfurth became a soul mate — over 80 years — far beyond the weekly trips, the honk of the horn under the bridges.

We were fortunate enough to have a hand in developing a major exhibition: "Charles C. Schweinfurth Uncompromising Architect of Cleveland's Valiant Age", sponsored by ARTneo: The museum of Northeast Ohio art and architecture, the Cleveland Public Library and Trinity Cathedral September 6, January 2014] Involvement in the discussions, examinations of texts and original drawings, workshops, visits and collection of raw data throughout Cleveland impressed upon each of us the aesthetic of one of Cleveland's significant architectural talents. "The significance and richness of his designs his ability to transform current design trends be it the earlier eastern Shingle style, the Richardsonian stone castle, the Tudor brick mansion, Gothic houses of worship and even his singular federalist design effort — into his own unique design statements, was unmatched by any of his contemporaries. His interiors were full of exuberance, richness and beauty. One cannot drive under the amazing stone and brick ridges of Rockefeller Park, or examine the intricate wood carvings of the choir pews at Trinity Cathedral, or glory in the interiors of the Cuyahoga County Courthouse without being in awe of his imagination and design skills."

Each time we enter a space, open or prepared, it becomes ours immediately.

David Shimotakahara in rehearsal with GroundWorks DanceTheater. Photo by Mark Horning.

Whether we ignore its impact, take it for granted, see what is special or unusual about it, or really engage with it, it leaves a mark. We are both in it and audience to it. We follow people in their spaces. And we follow them throughout the city. David Shimotakahara of Groundworks directs the use of space, its highs, middle and lows with the challenge that the audience understand the meaning of the movements. Sometimes it is mind tingling, other times enigmatic.

Minor White, a major photographer, former Professor of Photography at MIT, and editor of Aperture Magazine wrote about "The Secret of Looking". A photographer is always looking, so are we. We may see the same or very different things. Seeing may be as creative as making psychic contact with the play or dance. Writers and image-makers in film, a novel, or a poem create an environment within our environment and make us confront new perspectives, tangle ours with theirs, and leave memorable marks on our lives.

There are a number of places — physical spaces within which professionals and newly engaged performers have organized programs — in ways that we gain new perspectives, or simply enjoy old favorite plays. Especially ones that we have never been able to see before.

Cleveland Public Theater has stretched our minds within their complex, even though their space is –well, simply space. The single person –multiple part performances of every kind of battered body and soul still resonate years after. The simplest construction of chairs and tables ARE the set. Once, when the elevator was not working, Jim saw the upstairs performance; I saw the one on the level.

Dobama Theatre on Coventry. Photograph courtesy of Dobama Theatre.

It is helpful to understand even before attending where the playwright's or musician's, or choreographer's ideas are coming from but the resonance comes from the performances — of Ohio Ballet's *Blood Wedding*" and The Cleveland Play House's *The Crucible or* Karamu's memorable plays by Langston Hughes. The growth and struggles of all of the small theaters are forceful reminders of the power of writing, acting and directing. We have followed Victoria Bussart directing from the wonderful Playhouse Square theatres to Cain Park and Sarah May's talent from Karamu to Beck Center. We have met Dorothy and Reuben Silver at Karamu House, in the lower levels of Dobama's home in the basement of a building on Coventry Rd or in the renovated YMCA or at the Cleveland Play House. We have followed Eric Coble's playwriting talent, from Beck Center to the Allen Theater Ensemble's showcase of Faye Sholitan's new plays or Verb Ballet as it absorbed the cultures of the choreographers. We want to be able to think, dream, mull lines, movements, expressions — and the whole. There are people we have seen at many of these performances and it is like a group of cheerleaders. They appear in elevators, at the Farmer's Market, while taking a walk, delightfully by common interests and sometimes surprise. A hello, nod of greeting, rarely an engaged discussion.

One favorite moment is on the elevator at Playhouse Square, as 90+ year-old actress Dorothy Silver was emerging from her performance in Arthur Miller's *Crucible,* a memorable production. Dorothy is always memorable but we discussed the play, Arthur Miller and the performance, which was one of the finest we have ever seen at the CPL.

Once, when I was giving a workshop at the Cleveland Supplementary Education Center, an old warehouse building, I buzzed for the elevator and when the door opened, a student quartet, crunched for space, was rehearsing. We discussed the music they were "perfecting".

Elevators are important.

Iconic music, interesting music, old music, and new music have been part of our everyday lives. My heart is filled with Mozart; Jim loves opera. On wonderful evenings at home, or in the car, Jim and I listen to some of our favorite music daily. Many times it is quiet and graceful Scarlatti, or masterful mind-filling Handel. Julie Andrijuski landed on our doorstep, instrument in hand when she was a student at the Cleveland Institute of Music. More than a decade, graduation and marriage later she teaches music at Case Western Reserve, has major roles for Apollo's FIRE, Les Délices and several ensembles worldwide. What a way to be introduced to her specialties in baroque Music and Dance.

Les Délices artists (L-R): Julie Andrijeski, Debra Nagy. Photograph courtesy of Peter Nagy.

Les Délices artists (L-R) are: Julie Andrijeski, Emily Walhout, Michael Sponseller. Photography courtesy of Steven Mastroianni.

Apollo's Fire Staff Photo. Photography courtesy of Apollo's Fire

Apollo's Fire Staff Photo. Photography courtesy of Apollo's Fire

ChamberFest. Photography courtesy of ChamberFest Cleveland.

ChamberFest. Photography courtesy of ChamberFest Cleveland.

In the late 1980s and early 1990s we went behind the scenes, glimpsed into the life of opera singers who were here for their roles in mostly traditional operas performed by Lyric Opera Cleveland, but who sang in cities all over the world. Fontaine Follensbee had lead roles as Suzanna in Mozart's *Marriage of Figaro* and the world premiere of Libby Larsen's *Mrs. Dalloway*, a two-act chamber opera. These guests entered family life: Richard Clark was here when our dog was killed on Shaker Boulevard. Patti Jo Stevens had comic roles and we saw her again at Ohio Light Opera in Gilbert and Sullivan's *Yeomen of the Guard.*

We had climbed a thin wooden drop-down stair to a rooftop at the renovated Venetian blind factory, now a private home. The city and the west side world seen through our magnifying glass. Lake Erie was like a bowl of celery soup between housetops and we could hear and see a hovering helicopter over Metropolitan Hospital. I was always writing poetry in my mind. At the end of this day from the rooftop, the long shadows were like the venetian blinds that were made in the building originally. There were old peace stickers on the guardrail like silent pickets. I could look on the motorcycle shop where Scott would work to improve my four-wheel walker to make it safe many years later.

An unusual aspect of life with walkers, go-go carts, transport chairs and the like is the intimate knowledge of elevators, especially those back elevators off of restaurant kitchens, old, grand lifts in warehouses intended for huge and heavy moving, and, my favorite, the one in the original American Greetings Building now the 78th street home for dozens of artists' studios and galleries.

My favorite old elevator, complete with caged opening is in the Hay building of the Western Reserve Historical Society.

DANCECleveland in the early days when the Gibans children were taking classes at Cleveland Modern Dance.

In the 60s, Cleveland Modern Dance held dance classes attended by the Gibans children. Since its transformation into a presenting group, it has introduced Cleveland to the world's finest groups. We have seen almost every one since the 70s and feel resonance especially with Pilobolus, Mark Morris, Paul Taylor and the iconic Alvin Ailey carrying the river piece in our hearts.

DANCECleveland today. Ballet Biarritz © Olivier Houeix

Modern dance can be energetic, thoughtful, serious, fun, and stretch our imaginations as I am on stage with the dancers.

Jim studied with color theorist Josef Albers who wrote: "Color is the most relative medium in art. No one sees the same hue in the same way." [Introduction to *Interaction of Color,* 1963, Yale University Press] I studied with Rudolf Arnheim the visual psychologist; both experiences gave us spiritual alliance with Julian Stanzcak and Ed Mieczkowski whose work we honor daily in our living room. These mentors gave us background and visual permission. The discussion of our own living environment is discussed in a later section, but the resonance is with these encounters.

It used to be that we could look at art — on paper, on canvas, in the various media — leisurely. Today, there are openings practically every day. First, Second and Third Fridays, Thursdays lead. One can distill multiple perceptions at one or more galleries, meet the artists, go to their studios, see their work on-line, in hotels and hospitals. *CAN* (Collective Arts Network) *Journal Weekly* by blog and quarterly brings it all together from the Cleveland Museum of Art, MOCA Cleveland, Akron Art Museum, 78th Street Studios, the neighborhoods of Tremont, Gordon Square, Collinwood, Cleveland Heights, Chagrin Falls. It could be the biggest citywide ongoing art festival. A bewildering blast. The film buffs can see films at many of the same venues and create it in laboratories for filmmakers. Printmakers can look and learn with new Zygote-led opportunities at Waterloo in Collinwood. The most persistent and involved audiences can celebrate particular art forms such as glassmaking and the impact of important artists such as Cleveland Institute of Art Brent Kee Young, whose beautiful work resonates. This does not include the many wonderful exhibits by artists from all over the world.

This activity rumbles like a train going through. I want to take a deep breath.

What is really exciting is the focus on community and the arts. In less than a decade Collinwood, full of

German and Polish ethnic history, has won the struggle for manageable roads and sidewalks that had crumbled with age. The remarkable Waterloo Community is a blossoming garden of art activities, a sculpture park, and homes newly purchased by artists rising from the shambles around the iconic Beachland gathering hole where I listened to poets and music. New galleries led by the Maria Neil Art Program now mirror some of the steadiest methods to celebrate art such as exclusive art representation and exchange programs with other cities. Zygote Press' energetic leadership has expanded opportunities for starting, mid-career artists mentoring and encouraging newer artists at the Print Garage and Ink House. Cleveland art history would emphasize the importance of commercial lithography and art printmaking mid-century. This story includes a different context especially a strong supporting group, the Collinwood Development Corporation. It expands weekly, mirroring other bright spots around Cleveland — Superior, Gordon Square, Tremont, that have been building on the arts since the millennium.

The resonance rings throughout our beings. It may take time to sift into permanence, but the energy, leadership and will seems to be in place at this time.

Douglas Max Utter, *Cleveland Rain*, 2000 Oil on canvas, 8' x 9'. Photograph courtesy of the artist.

For us, it is the finding of soul-flooding work that has made the difference: our visit to Doug Max Utter's studio when we saw his wonderful ode to his mother as he paints a city bend in the road as he remembers her. The special moments with Master/Design Goldsmith Jim Mazurkewicz as he crafted an original piece of jewelry when I was filming the story of Potter and Mellen, where the legacy of regional metalwork was continuing, watching ChamberFest grow from clarinetist's Franklin Cohen's retirement from the Cleveland Orchestra into a thoroughly developed enhancement to the music scene, not unlike Jeannette Sorrells' Apollo's Fire decades ago or the more recent Les Délices of Debra Nagy. We were there at the beginning and relish the power of their leadership and stamina. We've watched them build programs and quality while we've traveled to their ever-changing venues. The churches envelop sound beautifully — a far cry from the first Apollo's Fire introduction at the Cedar Lee Theatre stage.

Libraries are the backbone of the community's intelligence. Our friend who lives with many issues concerning disability says she borrows the maximum thirty books when she can. She has said, "Books are my babies". I have said they are the last bastion of service orientation. The bastions of finding, my research projects could not progress without national book exchange, savvy Internet expertise and the enthusiasm of sharing holdings wherever they are.

The City in 1833, 1936. Mural by William Summer in the Brett Memorial Hall in the Cleveland Public Library. Photograph courtesy of the Cleveland Public Library.

Edwin Mieczkowski's mural for the Cleveland Public Library's Brett Hall Reading Room, *Sommer's Sun*, 1979. Photography courtesy of the Cleveland Public Library

Libraries lie deep in the soul of Cleveland.

Iconic artist, Edwin Mieczkowski climbed the Walker and Weeks stairs, with cane and seriously declining health, determined to interpret his mural in the Brett Reading Room of the Cleveland Public Library with a group of teachers, The "Silver Apples of the Moon " project (Shaker Heights Public Library, Cleveland Museum of Art and Cleveland Public Library in which the participant matched art and published poetry stimulated a Security Guard to slip into a workshop to present a Langston Hughes poem on a napkin at the Harvard Branch of the CPL; of the Carnegie-West branch of the CPL; at the Carnegie-West branch of the CPL, a workshop participant new to poetry, signed out all Mary Oliver's work. The area's longest ongoing poetry readings at the Shaker Heights Public Library have called on new and seasoned poets monthly. Daniel Thompson and I accompanied Loren Weiss, a newly retired businessman, to his first ever reading. Loren had asked how to get into the poetry "system"—he was a very fast learner and became the second Poet Laureate of Cleveland Heights within a few years. Sollace Kissell Hotze lived in Cleveland until her 100+ year-old father, a Jones Day partner died. We shared Laurel and Sarah Lawrence experiences and together developed *"Silver Apples of the Moon"*.

    Libraries keep the best regional secrets that are the heart of our regional culture. The donated original art, photographs, drawings and of course, books. They lay the foundation for our "culture". They are the spirit within our buildings; many have been lovingly renovated. Library public funding issues have always passed here. Jim's firm now owns the first branch of the Cleveland Public Library on West 25th Street. CPL has major holdings and commissions of regional art. The Cuyahoga County Public Library, especially its art-centered Mayfield Heights branch, and libraries in Cleveland Heights, Shaker Heights, Rocky River and Lakewood have been "homes away from home" for me and for the inter-generations of parents and children who grow together, children seeking school-needed research information, addicted borrowers and people who "take a deep breath" there. Libraries are the all-inclusive community we dream of having. Every project of mine has included communication with all of these, as well as the historical and archival libraries of the Western Reserve Historical Society and the universities and institutions around us. In addition, this rich and vast resource is hospitable to poets and writers and their needs. Currently there is leadership and collaboration on every writers' event. The Internet must have been invented with them in mind. Resonance and soul lurks on every shelf. Finding is what it is all about.

From the mid-century, Russell Atkins and Langston Hughes met at the main Cleveland Library and became friends, and Langston introduced Russell to publications that nurtured his early career. The architect Charles Schweinfurth archived his exemplary work of original drawings for Trinity Cathedral, his iconic building. The public housing archives are at Case Western Reserve –Kelvin Smith library; the detailed journals of Jeptha Wade, civic leader especially at University Circle are at the Western Reserve Historical Society. The Cuyahoga County Library system nurtures the writers especially. Choose a subject: art, botany, regional history, music, medicine and there is a library with fine resources to feed that inquiry. These stories that resonate with spirit and soul of place are the cornerstones of our life here.

Finding the portraits of Hart Crane by William Sommer and Frank Wilcox in the basement at the Kelvin Smith Library, the photographs of Ann and Bob Levine's Publix Book Mart at the Michael Schwartz Library at Cleveland State University and the original drawings for Shaker Towers at the Western Reserve Historical Society library – finding treasures that surface for the asking. Ask. These are samples of what belongs to all of us. There is the resonance of our city soul.

Ann and Bob Levine stewarded the gathering of books for our family over the years. Photography courtesy of the Michael Schwartz Library at Cleveland State University.

On the Fine Arts Garden, Cleveland
by Russell Atkins
The Poetry of Black America: Anthology of the 20th century

Oh the Fine Arts Garden, Cleveland
The Park's beautiful

Really
something so serious about it
serene and gloomy

mildly gloomy
mildly touching all things

softly

and pouring with

mellows the silver fountain

silver figures
more reposefully into the living shadows
and then the golden lamps

the while

slowly filtering—

Russell Atkins

Russell Atkins at 90

From an interview by Lolette Kuby, 1978 for FORUM:

Ten Poets of the Western Reserve, An Ohio Poets Series publication, The Poetry Forum Program, Mentor, Ohio. Through a grant from the Martha Holden Jennings Foundation

When and how did you begin writing poetry?
Why do you write?

I began writing poetry when I was eight or nine. It's very vague; I was eleven or twelve when I actually began to think of poetry as poetry. I started writing little plays. I had a number of teachers who encouraged me. One, Mrs. Martin, made some puppets that fascinated me. Then I made my own and wrote things for them to say — just lines, really. In junior high, my English teacher was interested in what I was doing and became my mentor. Under her influence, I began to write poems as such. She kept all I wrote and before she retired, she found them all and returned them to me. A lot of my poems are visually oriented. Most often I have a picture. Words come with the picture usually, but sometimes not. If the picture persists, I deliberately sit down and find words for it. But really, the initial moment of the poem is variable.

Biography

Russell Atkins grew up in Cleveland. He attended the Cleveland School of Art (now the Cleveland Institute of Art) and the Cleveland Institute of Music, and was Assistant to the Director of the Sutphen School of Music (1957-60). His musical works have been performed by members of the Cleveland Orchestra. In 1950, he founded and edited *Free Lance Magazine* and taught creative writing at Karamu House. Over the years, he has read his work at colleges and universities around the country and on radio and television, has participated in the writers' conferences and workshops and television productions. His books include *Phenomena* (1961), *Objects* (1963), *Heretofore* (1968), *Maleficium* (1971), and *Here In The* (1976). Now past 80, Russell Atkins still has the power to astonish. Though it has been some time since his last full book, he continues to post poems to the small presses of America.

The Revenge of Cleveland,
A Menu Against Nouvelle Cuisine

At a restaurant a la arboretum
in a trendy alley back of Harvard Square,
I sit down to a platter
of minimalist philosophy
and wait for more.
When none comes I realize
this IS the entrée, and it hits me, this will cost:
Three slivers of salmon looking for the life of them
like play-dough cut-outs, a spot of goose liver pate
nudged under a scrap of spinach grown probably
in a petri dish, a dash of tortellinis, that disgrace to pasta,
an upscale garnish of designer legumes, and,
existentially enough, a single olive
sans pimento – the whole dish could be
a display of new wave jewelry.

Enough of this 'less is more.'
More is more, and I want some.
Let's start with dumpling soup, the aroma buoyed
by globules of chicken fat, the hundred suns
that never shine on gray Cleveland.
Bring on the perogies, and put a tub of cheez-whiz
made from artificial imitation processed cheese-food
at one elbow, and at the other of mound of sauer kraut
steaming like the Cuyahoga stirred by a scow
of a spring morning. Egg noodles too, rolled and cut
and ladle by my heavy Slovenian great aunts.
Pumpernickel smeared with lard.
Give me a bellyful of kielbasa inspired indigestion
any day, a pile that makes you spout
'Lay on MacDuffski, and let no mouth cry, "Hold,
Enough!" To top it off, a roll of petica and
a quivering dollop of pick jelly salad

straight from the Stuckey's off the western pike
all frothed with non-dairy whip.

Enough of this light weight stuff
that lets you off to play squash or the stocks.
I want a heap of carbohydrates
so you can't move the rest of the afternoon
chowed down in a bar
with the Browns game blaring.
A meal as profound and murky
as an immigrant cathedral,
as bland and fulfilling as a busload of Slovenians
coming home from Polka Varieties
dreaming of Sunday dinner.

Ray McNiece

Chapter 6:
Our Collectables:
Sustaining Our Immediate Environment

In the late 1960's I was an "educator" at the Cleveland Museum of Art, really learning to look with my eyes and those of the people who I was charged with teaching or enlightening. Reading E.L. Konigsberg's masterful story of children at the Metropolitan Museum of Art, *The Mixed-Up Files of Mrs. Basil E. Frankenweiler Jr.* (1967), or using tape recorders to help pre-writers express their thoughts were used to engage growing children in my charge, but I was deeply engaged as well. The exhibition JUXTAPOSITIONS (1965) has held throughout my life. Designed before museums had transistor coaches, it created possibilities for involvement, discussion, and one's own life-long learning and teaching.

One of a dozen City Canvases commissions, developed by the Cleveland Area Arts Council — which Nina headed, NOVA and the Cleveland Growth Association in the 1970s. Story: Rejected by CSU for being too controversial.

We have feasted our eyes on walls all over the city. Our very favorite way is to go when we can really SEE the work, uninterrupted. That is very different from an "opening" scenario, when artists and viewers revel, many times talking mostly to one another. To be fair, those gatherings often bring students, artists, and old eyes to new works. At the millennium, it was possible to visit two or three openings on a weekend. With the momentum of arts growth since, there has been a concerted effort to stage openings strategically to keep the visitations manageable and lively. The scene has changed dramatically.

Original sculpture by Jim Gibans as a teenager.

Julian Stanczak *Carter Manor*, 1973 From the City Canvases project in the 1970s, which Nina spearheaded at the Cleveland Area Arts Council. The Carter Manor wall mural will be reconstructed by the 2018 FRONT International Cleveland Triennial.

The *CAN Journal* weekly blog of June 6, 2016 reported:

"...apart from the Cleveland Museum of Art turning 100 years old and still free, and apart from Devo front man Mark Mothersbaugh's exhibit Myopia sprawling from the Akron Art Museum to MOCA Cleveland, and apart from the many artists who call Cleveland home while they make an impact in other cities (like Dana Oldfather, whose exhibit of new paintings *Sweet Sweet Sweet is on view through July 2 at Zg Gallery in Chicago*), and apart from the summer festival season getting underway with Art By the Falls AND Parade the Circle, both this weekend, and apart from 19 artists making big impact along the RTA Redline by installing grand scale murals and photo-based work between the Airport and Tower City right now, and apart from new galleries (like 1299, which bills itself as "the first innovative fine arts gallery in full collaboration with nightlife entertainment") opening all the time, and apart from the fact that Bike Shaker is leading public art tours on bicycles, and that we have available far too many workshops and concerts to mention...."

Penny Rakoff, Nightscape on the Cuyahoga, #1, 1987. Ektacolor print, 14 3/4/' x 18 7/8". A favorite spot in Cleveland and a wonderful perspective.

One of Gloria's most poetic pieces.

In our hundreds of encounters with art and artists, we have enjoyed most watching those that change, develop depth, become...resonate with us, our past and present, as they give us strength, beauty, and insight.

Most of our artwork has been selected because a piece drew us to it. Many times, we would go to a gallery, explore the exhibition independently, and both reach one piece that "spoke" to each of us.

A few pieces have been commissioned to celebrate 5-year anniversaries or birthdays. These artists of choice have most usually become friends.

Fred Schmidt Dancing to 45/70. Commission for our 45th anniversary and Jim's 70th birthday.

Julian Stanzcak (Untitled – Carter Manor wall), Ed Mieczkowski (Untitled – Halle Building wall, (now the Wyndam Hotel), Phyllis Sloane, (Untitled – 17th street garage (now demolished) silk screen prints and Mort Epstein's "Plug" are part of the 12 @150 print City Canvases project. We became good friends when these were commissioned by the Cleveland Area Arts Council, American Institute of Architects, NOVA project in 1974. The prints, each so representative of the artist's work at the time, warms us with their presence. The stories of our relationship with these artists have been told in other sections.

Sometimes, the circumstances are unusual. Take our first purchase in the early 60s. We were on our way in to a movie at the old Continental Theater and one print caught our eye on the wall of the lobby. It was obviously historic, not in particularly good shape, but interesting enough that we followed up after the film, went to a print expert friend's apartment and asked if he thought it was worth risking $35.00. When we examined the history with the help of the curator of prints at the Cleveland Museum of Art, we found that we had a work by Romeyne de Hooghe the Etcher, "Entry of Louis the XIV into Dunkirk, 1700". The artist is well known but we have none in the Cleveland collection. Further and most recent research indicates that it is one part of a three-part large piece.

We had always wanted something by Joseph O'Sickey, whose home we stayed at in Deer Isle ME. He was prolific and his wonderful bright colorful paintings of gardens and interior living spaces were well known but usually too big for us to consider. His studio near Kent was full of early sketches and a life-story through his paintings and his circus figures, and animals.

Purchased at a benefit for the Cleveland Institute of Art from behind the bar. The first we could afford and fit in our space.

One time, we went to a benefit at the Cleveland Institute of Art. We wanted to support it but knew that the artworks would be beyond our budget. As we were getting a glass of wine, we saw "our O'Sickey", a small oil painting of an interior dressing room scene, full of his delightful happy colors—manageable. We knew if we even spoke, batted an eye, smiled, it would disappear.

Judith Salomon and Gibans vase. Secured straight from her studio.

Judith Salomon's bright colored, uniquely shaped vessels begged for a place in our front window—a terrific touch for a room that includes an archival Saarinen Womb chair (1945) that we inherited from my forward-looking father. Climbing the two-floor old sturdy staircase to the artist's studio, we saw her working environment and could put her in context — something that such visits accomplish. Our vessel, a shape only this artist might create, becomes the icon of that window.

Found in the gallery on Larchmere, perfect for our entry.

There was the day that Jim walked down to the short-lived outsider gallery on Larchmere where he found our unique full shelf-sized urban streetscape board sculpture by Michelangelo Lovelace. It is a perfect visual stopping place as people enter our home. His street signs are always engaging, but it is the clouds painted on the rooftops to the buildings that I talk about. Michelangelo had been a speaker on the Creative Essence panel so I knew how his career began and his struggles as it took shape.

Intrede van Lodewijk XIV in Duinkerke, 1658 to 1662, Romeyn de Hooghe, after Adam Frans van der Meulen, 1658-1700, Etching Early purchase from the lobby of the East Cleveland Theater for $35, one of a valued triptych by the artist in the 17th Century.

Fran Weintraub Lasky Woven Hanging. First commission for our 25th anniversary. Artist had a weaving gallery on Larchmere.

We started commissioning artists on our 20th anniversary. A floor to ceiling brightly colored wool hanging has been an important living room piece for 40 years. The weaving is simple but arranged with alternate tight classical and loosely woven cascading material that adds a warm touch to the room. The artist Fran Weintraub Lasky had a storefront weaving studio on Larchmere for a short time.

Fred Schmidt, sculptor, danced into our lives. Every five years over our sixty years of marriage, we have commissioned an artwork. It was our 45th anniversary and Jim's 70th birthday and our first sculpture commission. After our initial conversation, Fred went to work on a piece around which the living room "swings". It is bright red and many see a G clef or a g for Gibans. [Image: Dancing to 45/70, 1999, enamel on steel]*** It is a celebration of life and hope. (Just as his piece in white for the Cleveland Clinic Children's Hospital for Rehabilitation — a happenstance that Nina uses their therapeutic pool...)

On our 50th anniversary, we commissioned Chris Pekoc to create a double portrait. When designing portraits, Chris tries to represent who you are, as well as what you look like. In this work, he used drawing, photography, paint, written words (Jim's letter to my father asking to marry me, my poetry to him,) live flowers (including entwining stems), and gold leaf. A memorable six months of lively discussion, visitation to the studio, suggestions — 24 different possible photographs with 48 hand positions, frontal, and side-view facial images — and ideas bouncing everywhere followed. We headed to Bonfoey's where the owner joined in the discussion about the frame. The result is very special and well worth the effort and has resided since right above our bed. I had known Chris since the 70s when I was responsible for his commissioned work on Cleveland that is in the Brett Reading Room of the Cleveland Public Library. His museum quality work *Traversing Lake Erie* from the SPACES exhibition will always resonate — one of the most important representations of the spirit at the core of the city's industrial and water-dependent past.

Portrait of Nina and Jim Gibans from Chris Pekoc, commissioned on their 50th anniversary.

Christopher Pekoc *Traversing Erie: East Toward Buffalo, West Toward Cleveland*, 1999 Electrostatic print, shellac and gold leaf on polyester film, brass rivets and machine stitching. Photography courtesy of the Artist and Tregoning and Company. First seen at SPACES.

Several works by the same artist allows us to look at their careers in greater depth and enjoy their development as artists.

Phyllis Sloane moved from her magnificent Tudor house on Fairmount Blvd. to the twelfth floor of our high-rise. We honor her memory with a work in the public hallway — a portion of a triptych of the building and scene across the street. But her distinctive sense of color, pattern, mass and line is perhaps seen best in her still life arrangements or portraits, mostly of her family or people we know. So in the bathroom, living room, bedroom we meet and greet family members like the friends they were.

One of a dozen City Canvases commissions, developed by the Cleveland Area Arts Council — which Nina headed, NOVA and the Cleveland Growth Association in the 1970s. Photograph courtesy of Kristina Reagan.

Michael Loderstedt is still a force as a leader in the art college at Kent State University. He is a mentor, collaborator, and distinguished individual artist whose work plums the depth of his heritage and our environs. First prize winner of the last juried "May Show" — a momentary reprise, in the late 90s, his recent community roles and commissions have been especially noteworthy.

Our five Loederstadt holdings include a collage based on our family images that we commissioned, his "G" from the Bestiary screen-print collagraph executed with colleague Craig Lucas that greets people as they enter our home, and 3.29.1998, 5:00pm @41.34'26"N, memorializing the closing of the Busta Gallery in 1998 in precise nautical terms. A small poetry book *18 Gardens and their Gardeners,* a series of photographs by Loederstadt of the "secret" rooftop gardens, including Jim's at Shaker Towers, commemorates the stories of these residents. The poems reflect the stories told by the gardeners.

On our 60th anniversary, we commissioned a work by Amy Casey, a joyful artist out of the Cleveland Institute of Art, who was a Cleveland Arts Prize winner in 2009, the same year as Nina's award. She summarized our careers and joy of Cleveland through a design that wove the Old Arcade, Severance Hall, Lakeview Terrace, The Cleveland Museum Of Art, all places that have engaged us for many, many hours — a wonderful life summary.

We have tired of very few of our art works. We serve food on George Roby's platter, or put nuts in Ed Winter's candy dish. We travel our hall and five rooms and they have become one with us. Each work brings lasting pleasure and good stories. We have found them all over town: at the Folk Art Gallery and The Verne Gallery in Little Italy; Design Corner and Heights Art in Cleveland Heights, Bonfoeys and CSU Galleries downtown, Tregoning and Company and Hilary Gent at 78th Street, Tremont galleries. A recent purchase at the gallery at Ursuline College by Thomas Salomon, who we have yet to know, from "In Memoriam: Responses to the Unanswerable" and "Sun Solution" by A.D. Peters an oil on steel slate are among our most poignant works.

William Busta. Photography Courtesy of the Collective Arts Network

We treasure most our "relationships" with clairvoyant advisors like Bill Busta that led to deep appreciation of many artists like H. Carroll Cassill and Laurence Channing. We have been waiting for the moment to purchase a work by Douglas Max Utter. As with several artists, some things we would have considered because we were so drawn to them have been too large or too expensive. We are now limited by wall space, but carry images we have and see. What better vision than resonance and renewed understanding. We got to know Rob Mihaly when he started SPACES in a small room at 1375 Euclid, the building that now houses WCPN and WVIZ Ideastream, and WCLV. We own two of his raku pots, reminding me daily of his role in being at the right place at the right time. SPACES has renovated a new home in Hingetown, not far from locations 2 and 3 in downtown Cleveland. Daniel Hodermarsky was a friend, neighbor and beloved teacher at the Cleveland Supplementary Education Center, the old warehouse that was used by the Cleveland Public Schools for art in the 70s. Robert Little's geodesic dome building for the Cleveland Public School System that has been a nature center and administration building over the years. We own two small works: An abstract oil painting from the 60s was done about the same time as the wall construction of painted wood and metal that he gave us when he left Cleveland to teach at Deerfield Academy. We attended his wake on Deer Isle in Maine when he died and joined several dozens of his students for a kielbasa-fest to celebrate him properly.

We have recently re-connected with Lisa Hodermarsky who grew up with our daughters and has been a curator at the Yale Museum of Art. Our children studied with Trudy Wiesenberger, George Roby, and Phyllis Sloane's daughter Lisa. The connections never really end.

The artist Douglas Max Utter with his work at the Busta Gallery. Photograph courtesy of Jim Lang.

We can also contemplate the extraordinary meaning of camaraderie for artists of the Cleveland School who taught together inside the building and at summer places, Brandywine, Berlin Heights or even Monhegan Isle in ME. Their influences are palatable today; the resonance is there when we trace their work, journals, and the work of their students. One does not need every stone on the path, but we fill in the gaps with joy. Frank Wilcox, Henry Keller all the way to the work of my aunt who knew Alex Warshawsky and studied with Paul Travis.

One of the most valuable reasons for collecting is to capture (in a home) the artist's persona — the changes in media, the subjects, the colorations. Over the years, they join the family. Many works will indeed go to one of our children's homes, resonance with our life and theirs and Cleveland.

Frank Wilcox — one of the important icons of Cleveland art history, and the Cleveland School of Art. Frank Wilcox, courtesy of Bonfoey Gallery.

Look with me at the images paired for these purposes:

The Troubadour, 1868-1873. Honoré Daumier (French, 1808-1879). Oil on fabric; framed: 99.5 x 73 x 8 cm (39 1/8 x 28 11/16 x 3 1/8 in.); unframed: 83.6 x 56.8 cm (32 7/8 x 22 5/16 in.). The Cleveland Museum of Art, Bequest of Leonard C. Hanna, Jr. 1958.23

Harpist, mid 700s. North China, Tang dynasty (618-907). Glazed earthenware; overall: h. 32.1 cm (12 5/8 in.). The Cleveland Museum of Art, Edward L. Whittemore Fund 1931.450

Shepherds in a Round Dance, around 1500. Netherlands, early 16th century. Tapestry weave: wool and silk; overall: 360.5 x 401.1 cm (141 7/8 x 157 7/8 in.). The Cleveland Museum of Art, Gift of Leonard C. Hanna, Jr., for the Coralie Walker Hanna Memorial Collection 1939.158

Studious Sketcher, 1945. Milton Avery (American, 1885-1965). Oil on canvas; framed: 107 x 86.7 x 6.3 cm (42 1/8 x 34 1/8 x 2 1/2 in.); unframed: 91.4 x 71.1 cm (35 15/16 x 27 15/16 in.). The Cleveland Museum of Art, Contemporary Collection of The Cleveland Museum of Art 1967.94 © Milton Avery Trust / Artists Rights Society (ARS), New York

Portrait of a Woman as Diana, 1752. Jean-Marc Nattier (French, 1685-1766). Oil on canvas; framed: 127.5 x 107.5 x 10 cm (50 3/16 x 42 5/16 x 3 7/8 in.); unframed: 100.4 x 79.5 cm (39 1/2 x 31 1/4 in.). The Cleveland Museum of Art, Bequest of John L. Severance 1942.643

Nathaniel Hurd, c. 1765. John Singleton Copley (American, 1738-1815). Oil on canvas; framed: 90.5 x 78 x 6.5 cm (35 5/8 x 30 11/16 x 2 1/2 in.); unframed: 76.2 x 64.8 cm (30 x 25 1/2 in.). The Cleveland Museum of Art, Gift of the John Huntington Art and Polytechnic Trust 1915.534

Walt Whitman, 1887-88. Thomas Eakins (1844-1916). Oil on canvas, 30 1/8 x 24 1/4 in. (76.5 x 61.6 cm.), 1917.1. Courtesy of Philadelphia Museum

Portrait of a Woman, c. 1917-1918. Amedeo Modigliani (Italian, 1884-1920). Oil on canvas; framed: 94.6 x 77.4 x 6 cm (37 3/16 x 30 1/2 x 2 5/16 in.); unframed: 65 x 48.3 cm (25 9/16 x 19 in.). The Cleveland Museum of Art, Gift of the Hanna Fund 1951.358

Portrait of a Woman, c. 1665. Gerard Terborch (Dutch, 1617-1681). Oil on canvas; framed: 87.5 x 77 x 7 cm (34 7/16 x 30 5/16 x 2 3/4 in.); unframed: 63.3 x 52.7 cm (24 7/8 x 20 11/16 in.). The Cleveland Museum of Art, The Elisabeth Severance Prentiss Collection 1944.93

Portrait of George Pitt, First Lord Rivers, c. 1768-1769. Thomas Gainsborough (British, 1727-1788). Oil on canvas; framed: 261 x 181 x 9 cm (102 3/4 x 71 1/4 x 3 1/2 in.); unframed: 234.3 x 154.3 cm (92 3/16 x 60 11/16 in.). The Cleveland Museum of Art, Gift of the John Huntington Art and Polytechnic Trust 1971.2

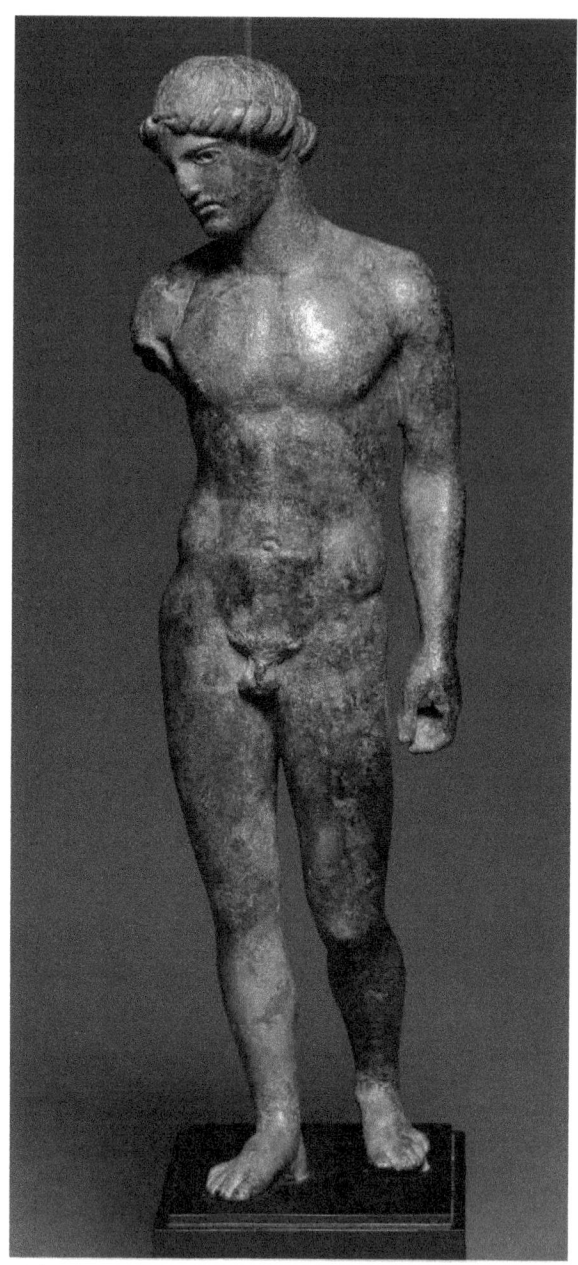

Athlete Making an Offering, c. 450-425 BC. Greece, probably from workshop of Locri or Tarentum, Classical Period. Bronze; overall: h. 21 cm (8 1/4 in.); without tang: h. 19.8 cm (7 3/4 in.). The Cleveland Museum of Art, Gift of the Hanna Fund 1955.684

Youth (From Chateau de Chaumont Set), 1512-1515. France, Lyon(?), early 16th century. Silk and wool; tapestry weave; overall: 321.8 x 452 cm (126 11/16 x 177 15/16 in.). The Cleveland Museum of Art, John L. Severance Fund 1960.176.2

Portrait of the Ladies Amabel and Mary Jemima Yorke, c. 1761. Joshua Reynolds (British, 1723-1792). Oil on canvas; framed: 224.4 x 201.2 x 11.4 cm (88 5/16 x 79 3/16 x 4 1/2 in.); unframed: 196 x 170 cm (77 1/8 x 66 7/8 in.); former: 223.5 x 198 x 9 cm (87 15/16 x 77 15/16 x 3 1/2 in.). The Cleveland Museum of Art, Bequest of John L. Severance 1942.645

A Bridal Couple, c. 1470. Southern Germany, 15th century. Oil on panel; framed: 77.5 x 51 x 8 cm (30 1/2 x 20 1/16 x 3 1/8 in.); unframed: 62.3 x 36.5 cm (24 1/2 x 14 5/16 in.). The Cleveland Museum of Art, Delia E. Holden and L. E. Holden Funds 1932.179

Mourning Saint John and Mourning Virgin (pair), c. 1250-1275. Spain, Kingdom of Castile and Leon, 13th century. Polychromed oak; overall: 154.9 x 36.8 x 20.3 cm (60 15/16 x 14 1/2 x 8 in.). The Cleveland Museum of Art, Gift of Mr. and Mrs. Francis F. Prentiss 1930.621

Time and Again, 1994. Joy Jacobs (American, 1932-2004). Gouache; sheet: 27.3 x 36.9 cm (10 11/16 x 14 1/2 in.). The Cleveland Museum of Art, Gift of Nina and James Gibans in honor of Tom Hinson and his devotion to artists in the community 2012.46

Lot's Wife, 1989. Anselm Kiefer (German, 1945-). Oil paint, ash, stucco, chalk, linseed oil, polymer emulsion, salt and applied elements (e.g., copper heating coil), on canvas, attached to lead foil, on plywood panels; framed: 350 x 410 cm (137 3/4 x 161 3/8 in.). The Cleveland Museum of Art, Leonard C. Hanna Jr. Fund 1990.8.a
© Anselm Kiefer

REVISITING A WORK OF ART
Lot's Wife by Anselm Kiefer, Cleveland Museum of Art

1.
Crumpled in a fist of fire
the world cries
for what it could possibly have done to itself
to sacrifice its essence.
How did it prepare?
play with fireworks? look through a barrel?
carry a gun?, spit out bastard words
into sprawl spilling hate?
Why don't we know so we will always know
so our children will not have to ask?

2.
I am lost in the browned meadow
no marked paths, no marked turns,
houses no one sees were homes
peeling chimneys, faded carpets unused rooms.
best at sunset in the rosy light.
all houses are one house
history splays into dust.
stories wrap around buildings and people.
distant cousins known only by captions
Whose family do I share in my family?
Where are we? By the roadside?
In the rubble? On the field?

3.
This cocoon of dust
for souls
and butterflies next spring
for the cayenne spotted meadow
will grow one red flower for each
to take a long drink into history.
replenish hope
and remember the forgotten.

—NFG

The Kitchen Garden at La Brunié, 1941. Jacques Villon (French, 1875-1963). Oil on canvas; unframed: 65 x 92 cm (25 9/16 x 36 3/16 in.). The Cleveland Museum of Art, Leonard C. Hanna, Jr. Fund 1964.95 © Artists Rights Society (ARS), New York

Gardener's House at Antibes, 1888. Claude Monet (French, 1840-1926). Oil on fabric; framed: 91.1 x 118.4 x 13.6 cm (35 13/16 x 46 9/16 x 5 5/16 in.); unframed: 66.3 x 93 cm (26 1/16 x 36 9/16 in.). The Cleveland Museum of Art, Gift of Mr. and Mrs. J. H. Wade 1916.1044

Wooded and Hilly Landscape, 1660s. Jacob van Ruisdael (Dutch, 1628/29-1682). Oil on canvas; framed: 73 x 81.5 x 11 cm (28 11/16 x 32 1/16 x 4 5/16 in.); unframed: 51.6 x 59.4 cm (20 5/16 x 23 3/8 in.). The Cleveland Museum of Art, Leonard C. Hanna, Jr. Fund 1963.575

Mount Sainte-Victoire, c. 1904. Paul Cézanne (French, 1839-1906). Oil on fabric; framed: 87.5 x 106.5 x 7 cm (34 7/16 x 41 7/8 x 2 3/4 in.); unframed: 72.2 x 92.4 cm (28 3/8 x 36 3/8 in.). The Cleveland Museum of Art, Bequest of Leonard C. Hanna, Jr. 1958.21

Thirty-Six Immortal Poets, mid 1700s. Attributed to Tatebayashi Kagei (Japanese). Two-fold screen; ink, color, and gold on paper; image: 170 x 182.8 cm (66 7/8 x 71 15/16 in.); overall: 174.4 x 187.2 cm (68 5/8 x 73 11/16 in.); closed: w. 94 cm (37 in.). The Cleveland Museum of Art, Mr. and Mrs. William H. Marlatt Fund 1960.183

The Surge, 1958. Conrad Marca-Relli (American, 1913-2000). Oil and collage on canvas; unframed: 137.1 x 180.3 cm (53 15/16 x 70 15/16 in.). The Cleveland Museum of Art, Contemporary Collection of The Cleveland Museum of Art 1960.58

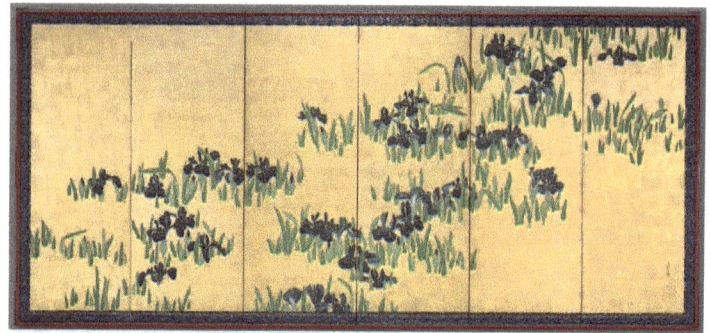

Irises, 1700s. Watanabe Shiko (Japanese, 1683-1755). Pair of six-panel folding screens, ink and color on gilded paper; overall: 154 x 334.3 cm (60 5/8 x 131 9/16 in.). The Cleveland Museum of Art, Gift of The Norweb Foundation 1954.603

Water Lilies (Agapanthus), c.1915-1926. Claude Monet (French, 1840-1926). Oil on canvas; framed: 204.9 x 430.3 x 6 cm (80 5/8 x 169 3/8 x 2 5/16 in.); unframed: 201.3 x 425.6 cm (79 1/4 x 167 1/2 in.). The Cleveland Museum of Art, John L. Severance Fund and an anonymous gift 1960.81

River and Mountains on a Clear Autumn Day, c. 1624-1627. Dong Qichang (Chinese, 1555-1636). Handscroll, ink on Korean paper; painting only: 38.4 x 136.8 cm (15 1/16 x 53 13/16 in.). The Cleveland Museum of Art, Purchase from the J. H. Wade Fund 1959.46

Head of Amenhotep III Wearing the Blue Crown, c. 1391-1353 BC. Egypt, New Kingdom, Dynasty 18, reign of Amenhotep III. Granodiorite; overall: 39.1 x 30.3 x 27.7 cm (15 3/8 x 11 7/8 x 10 7/8 in.). The Cleveland Museum of Art, Gift of the Hanna Fund 1952.513

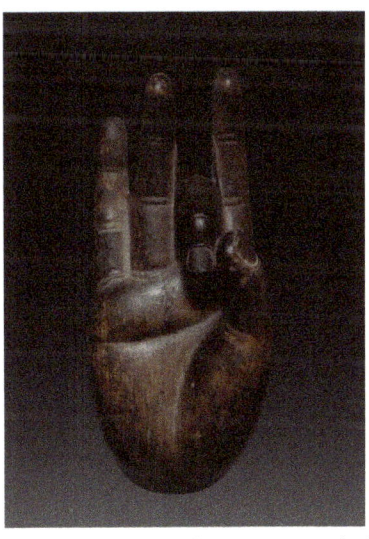

Hand of Buddha, 710-794. Japan, late Nara Period (710-794). Wood; overall: 40 cm (15 11/16 in.). The Cleveland Museum of Art, The Norweb Collection 1956.126

Adam and Eve (pair of statuettes), c. 1535. Daniel Mauch (German, 1477-1540). Boxwood; overall: 18.3 x 7 x 4 cm (7 3/16 x 2 3/4 x 1 9/16 in.). The Cleveland Museum of Art, Purchase from the J. H. Wade Fund 1946.429

Adam and Eve, 1504. Albrecht Dürer (German, 1471-1528). Engraving; sheet: 25.2 x 19.4 cm (9 7/8 x 7 5/8 in.); image: 25 x 19.2 cm (9 13/16 x 7 1/2 in.). The Cleveland Museum of Art, Dudley P. Allen Fund 1944.473

Chapter 7:
Affect and Effect

Loganberry Bookstore. Photography courtesy of Terry Michelle.

Mac's Backs Paperbacks whose support for regional writers has been monumental.

The strength of the leadership of those civic leaders who, almost exactly 100 years ago pulled together their wisdom and resources (many times personal), gave us the legacies for a sustainable city. They were the developers of substantial ideas such as department stores, Metroparks, libraries, museums, cemeteries and houses of worship, health, welfare and educational institutions. Many have grown to lead to national and world stature. We feel their presence every day and have a sense of their "condition". On the other hand, the lure of a place where small businesses could grow, ideas could flourish, attracted people from all over the world to a city on the rise. Those folks gave us our tradesmen, experts in particular crafts, manual abilities, and sense of "materials". They gravitated to parts of the city where people spoke their languages and populated neighborhood bookstores, hardware stores, mom and pop men's and women's garment shops and filled our shopping areas and arcade spaces. All of this leaves a resonance that is palpable as we glory in some of the spaces and seek to fill many empty storefronts.

We have been most connected to the arts scene. When we assess the early histories of the Cleveland School of Art, we are in awe of their faculty camaraderie and inter-relationships. If it had not been for the communication among and between the earliest geniuses, Henry Keller, Frank Wilcox, Paul Travis, Abel and Alex Warshawsky, Marguerite and William Zorach, Charles Burchfield, William Sommer, with their long teaching tenures, walks all over Cleveland and Ohio, writings from their travels and stints in New York and other locations, we could not even contemplate their legacies. Not to mention their decades of exhibitions at the Cleveland Museum of Art annual May Shows and at the few local galleries. Their communal spirit sustained them. They provide the foundation for discussions today for their work is mostly in homes and is preserved in stalwart galleries. They ARE the Soul of Cleveland's art. But they also built the framework for the Cleveland Institute of Art, launching it upon its next era in the Albert Kahn building, originally built to construct aircraft during World War II.

Commercial printmaking here was known and ordered all over the country. Although there were clusters of printmakers over the century, the art of printmaking today is growing through opportunity and mentoring.

Frank Wilcox. "Jeun Homme Avec Chapeau", n.d. (drawing of Hart Crane) Kelvin Smith Library Special Collections & Archives, Case Western University.

Cleveland Institute of Art Building on Magnolia.

The new George Gund Building, Cleveland Institute of Art.
Photograph courtesy of Robert Muller/Cleveland Institute of Art.

Maltz Performing Arts Center at the Temple-Tifereth Israel on the campus of Case Western Reserve University. Photography courtesy of MGA Partners, Architects.

Writing the book: *The Community Arts Council Movement: History, Opinions and Issues* gave me the long perspective on making a difference and community action in the arts. Usually the sun and moon must be in alignment. When people, the timing, and the opportunities line up, there is a wonderful synergism that takes form. In the 70s, there was a Cleveland Area Arts Council which I headed. This group connected artists with the community in as many ways as we could. Programmatically, they were artists of 12 City Canvases, commissions in the Cleveland Public Library, poetry in the Playhouse Square theaters, and Education for Aesthetic Awareness taught by teams of arts faculties and given credit at four colleges and Universities. There were important organizational ideas that were stimulated, and we learned a lot from what was being tried in many other cities and counties. Some of these ideas, while stimulating to the participants, were too new to this community. There was no public or private interest in pulling the pieces together that would make a substantial difference for artists and arts organizations, especially the smaller ones. The timing was not right. But discussions were beginning and increased as the idea of community support could develop and take hold. About a decade later, a broadly based Cuyahoga Arts and Culture organization could purposefully do the studies, research and build on possibilities for the proper and ongoing funding base for the arts with the broad mission to inspire and strengthen the community by investing in arts and culture. Inspire it did, and what started in 2006 as the first success in approving a tax on cigarettes was extended in 2015 to 2027. **Everyone** was on board — a sympathetic county government and foundation system. It took two tax initiatives and everyone on board — arts, of course, but foundations, corporations, sports organizations and many many committed volunteers. The programmatic ideas have been a natural outcome of their planning, which laid the groundwork for what Cleveland has today—solid systems for civic action and proper attention to the issues affecting the arts and artists. The soul of the city's arts is embedded in this development, giving sustenance to creative excellence since the 70s. The roles of the Ohio Arts Council, Cleveland and George Gund Foundations and their boards have provided backbone to these efforts by picking them up by the scruff of their necks and placing them on stable footing by providing the models for management stability. This has stimulated growth and support for arts organizations large and small, artists in all phases of their development, and made sure that there is diversity and equal handedness.

These elements all developed almost simultaneously with molding and expert advisors. Timing and synergism, the people whose talents and expertise could expedite planning and implementation worked together! The community had much to build on, and new leadership developed.

Other important aspects of sustainability:

The growth and ongoing sustainability and excellence of the Cleveland Orchestra, the breathtaking environments for listening at University Circle's Severance Hall, the Cleveland Institute of Music's Mixon Hall and new Milton and Tamir Maltz Performing Arts Center. The renovation, expansion, or new additions and stewardship of missions and buildings. At the same time, as well as the Playhouse Square's five spectacular venues: The Palace, State, Ohio, Allen and Hanna. We grew up listening at Cleveland's churches and Temples, places for peace and participation.

One of the Samuel Freedlander Memorial Lecture Series on free speech given by Floyd Abrams, 2017. Occasion was the annual City Club of Cleveland meeting of 2017. Photograph courtesy of Michelangelo's Photography.

The proliferation of visual arts opportunities – the Northeast Ohio area once had a twig of galleries; it is now an area-wide "museum" with options for viewing, comparing and collecting from large and small galleries as if were one extended museopolis. This development, all over the region, has been accompanied by a collective voice for the Visual Arts. After several attempts to find a proper way to serve galleries, museums, art schools and colleges including non-profit and for-profit businesses, The Collective Arts Network and the *CAN Quarterly* journal under the stewardship of Michael Gill, its editor, has achieved that goal with a comprehensive high quality "global portrait" available free at more than 200 locations including hotel rooms.

On November 1, 2001, Radio Seaway donated commercial radio station WCLV-FM (104.9 FM) to the non-profit WCLV Foundation. Radio Seaway partners Robert Conrad and Rich Marschner arranged the transaction in response to what they and others felt was a disturbing trend in larger radio markets — corporate buyouts of traditionally classical commercial stations, with the new owners invariably discontinuing the format. In addition to assuring the continuation of the classical music format, the transfer of commercial station WCLV-FM to the non-profit WCLV Foundation provided funding via the station's "excess profits" for local arts organizations: the Cleveland Orchestra, the Cleveland Institute of Music, the Cleveland Museum of Art, the Cleveland Play House, and the Cleveland Foundation. On August 10, 2010, WCLV announced it would move from its long-time "Radio Ranch" studios in Warrensville Heights to the Idea Center at Playhouse Square in Downtown Cleveland, home to area PBS member WVIZ and NPR member WCPN. The station's transmitter site remains in Avon. The move occurred in December 2010. On May 4, 2011, Radio Seaway announced it was donating WCLV to WVIZ and WCPN's owner, Ideastream. Under the terms of the deal, Cleveland Classical Radio, which has long operated the station on behalf of Radio Seaway, continued to operate the station until November 1, 2012, the 50th anniversary of the WCLV intellectual unit. On that date, WCLV officially became part of Ideastream.

The City Club of Cleveland has been part of our family since mid-century, with two of us serving on its Board. With a national reputation as a "citadel of free speech," the City Club's 100-year commitment to informing, connecting and motivating citizens has secured its place in history as a vital center for community debate. It digs deeply into community and world-vital issues.

The result of the work of all of these groups is that there is major collaboration among them, and creative thinking is welcomed and manageable for almost every program. That IS the city's sustaining voice. It resonates loudly.

The effect of these efforts has had a profound impact on us and on a community proud of its assets.

Cleveland Orchestra. Photograph courtesy of Roger Mastroianni.

A serious haven. See University Circle: creating a sense of place. Photograph courtesy of Roger Mostrianni.

Epilogue

How fortune plays into a lifespan – A path of being able to follow passions, treat but not diminish disabilities, look at the world with hope. Early interaction with people across the city — educators, artists, civic leaders, health professionals and old friends who have stayed here and with mentors everywhere who encouraged rather than discouraged risk. In case you worry that we have been too insular, we watch every pitch, basketball game and especially tennis from the time major tennis was played on courts at Roxboro School in Cleveland Heights. My father was a city tennis champion on the courts at Rockefeller Park but we did not know it until after he died.

The diverse needs of any city challenge everyone. They are about inequality, diversity, caring and doing.

We started the Soul of Cleveland project by asking questions at a table full of diverse people. The surveys and events got more people thinking about our common lives. The ways we found sustainability took digging into 60-80 years of living.

We ask more questions of ourselves and the community: What has made a difference in your perspective on life? What are some things that resonate and sustain it?

Eric Coble in the lobby of WCLV. Cleveland should give him a great big hug, and cheered the many theaters that have produced his work.

The Hunchback of Notre Dame at Great Lakes Theater. Photograph courtesy of Great Lakes Theater. Directed by Victoria Bussert.

Dorothy Silver at Dobama. A lifetime of poignancy and personal mentoring. Photograph courtesy of Peter Larson.

- Responses can only be real. We went to a new play in 2016 on one of the city's most challenging times — Hough Riots, in many ways in the background for remaining issues today in the black community. We lived through those days, participated vigorously in the integration of Shaker Heights, live in a condominium built to assure diversity. It was like not being Lithuanian enough in the 70s. The discussion in the theater was difficult for those who were not THERE in terms of the hatred, the bias, the poverty, the family breakdown, the landscape that was eviscerated. What is the best way to build confidence in solutions? Will it demand a different kind of caring and confidence? Dorothy Silver, whose memorable acting in The Cleveland Play House production of Arthur Miller's *The Crucible* and Beck Center for the Art's production of Eric Coble's *The Velocity of Autumn* goes to the heart of what we mean by sustainability, comments on Karamu and the

"soul" of the institution begun 100 years ago with a vision of a community of people with projects that allowed everyone to grow together.
- One of the most frustrating moments was our interface with Icabod Flewellen who wanted so much a museum of African American Art for his extensive collection. His dream never truly materialized even though lots of people made yeoman efforts to help. He would not accept the help that he needed. Fortunately, the East Cleveland Public Library has archived his collection and his year celebrated this 100th birthday. A generation later, there are young minority artists with strong voices and talent who have not found ways to flourish. CPAC has been inclusive but...what more is needed to give confidence? According to their teachers and mentors, the strongest have left the city to pursue their own talents.

The people and moments with resonance have resounded loudly in our lives. We wonder
- What happens next to the wonderful young talent found by the Cleveland School of the Arts? Cleveland Public Theater? West Side Theatre? Do we all see/hear/understand it?
- What has been the affect upon the deaf community of Signstage Theater?
- What about the effect on other disabled individuals of Dancing Wheels?
- What about the role of the Arts in sustaining the city with resonance and meaning?
- Where is Cleveland in the global picture?

The Cavalier's victories are energizing for today. It has been a joy to watch the change when there is synergism and everything and everyone comes together. The huge poster of individual achievement will last only so long. It will take more than winning sports teams although that is a place to start. The work of those of international achievement and excellence in music, art, literature, theater, and dance should have the same public attention. The Cleveland Arts Prize has brought local recognition to some achievers of all ages for many decades, but the audience is an ensemble of admirers. The biographies and films are excellent, but we have to know how to look for them. When someone is published outside of the city, performs on the stages of the world, has a building acknowledged for its excellence elsewhere, a play performed on Broadway or in Tokyo it is a celebration for all of us. We do not need a committee to tell us. Register it all year. Find a way to show it on YouTube, read it by a link. I want to know. I want to hear the music, laugh the laugh, follow the work, read the words. This does not happen on the street or in fairs and festivals, but celebrates with equal public notice as sports heroes. List them once a month, like an honor role. Could the Cleveland Arts Prize take this on across the arts? A place to deliver the news or message would give incentive to groups like LitCleveland, Zygote Press, CAN journal, and others whose work reaches broadly and to individuals across the arts. Work of excellence has a common language. It must be shared. Collectively, it resonates. It sustains us.

The spirit of inclusion may be developing. Renaissance may have begun at the renovation of our major public space which took years and persistence and the right leadership.

There is hope that in the years to come, the community will understand its needs and map out manageable solutions to the inequalities of all kinds that are very real. The Soul

Appendices
Bibliography

The following lists were developed upon discussions in the early stages of the Soul of Cleveland.

PUBLICATIONS
Barbara Tanner Angell, *The Long Turn Towards Light*, Cleveland State University Poetry Center, 1978.
ARTneo Catalog 2014: *Charles F. Schweinfurth: Uncompromising Architect of Cleveland's Valiant Age*.
Russell Atkins *Here In The,* Cleveland State University Poetry Center 1976.
Gaston Bachelard: *The Poetics of Space,* 1958.
Ernest Braun and David Cavagnaro *Living Water,* American West Publishing Co. 1971.
Cleveland Public Library, *The Art, Architecture and Collections of the Main Library: A Self-Guided Tour 1999.*
Cleveland Urban Design Collaborative: *Urban Infill*, volume no 1: *Cities Growing Smaller,* volume no 2:

Pop Up City; volume number 3: Watercraft; volume no 4: *Cleveland Stories: True until Proven Otherwise*; volume no.5: *Diagrammatically*; volume no. 6: *Coldscapes: Design Ideas for Winter Cities*; volume no.7: *Historic Preservation and Urban Change.*

Committee for Public Art: *A Walking Tour and Guide to Public Art in Downtown Cleveland* 1995.

Jim Cox, *Cleveland's Public Sculpture,* TIMELINE: A publication of the Ohio Historical Society, April-June 2014.

Mike DeCapite*: Through the Windshield,* Sparkle Street Books, 1998.

Russell Duino: *The North Coast Book Trade 1819 to the Present.*

David Giffels*: The Hard Way on Purpose,* Scribner, 2014.

Laura C. Gooch: *The Doan Brook Handbook: A Guide to the Shaker Lakes, Rockefeller Park, the Cleveland Cultural Gardens and Points Between*, The Nature Center at Shaker Lakes, 2001.

Philip Kaplan: *The Making of a Collector: Laukhuff's of Cleveland,* Northern Ohio Bibliophilic Society, Akron, 1990.

Editor Maj Raigan: *The Big Book of Daniel: Collected Poems of Daniel Thompson,* Bottom Dog Press 2011.

Ray McNiece: *The Lives of A Poet* February 2015, Cleveland Public Theater.

Mary Oliver: "Wild Geese", *Dream Works* 1986.

Terry Tempest Williams: *An Unspoken Hunger: Stories From the Field.*

David Young: *Seasoning: A Poet's Year*, Oberlin OH.

SUGGESTED CDs and DVDs

Hildur Asgeidoilthir Jonson — Fiberwork Process in studio.

Les Délices — Myths and Allegories.

Daniel Thompson — Drumplay 2, "Under the Map of the World Where I Sleep" and Readings.

John Richmond — The Mercurys with Hollywood Slim.

Michael Doc Dreyfuss with Dave Morrison — *Nice and Queasy*.

A Citadel of Free Speech since 1912-The Cleveland City Club.

Florence Mustric — *organ* East of Berlin.

Gene's Hot Jazz *HOT*.

Russell Atkins – Nina Giban Interview.

Water Soul of Cleveland.

VIDEOS by Nina Gibans

University Circle: Creating a Sense of Place.

The History of Potter and Mellen. Produced by Mark Wade Stone.

Robert A. Little: The Vision of Pepper Ridge Rd.

The People Puzzle: The Impact of Prejudice on Children — Cleveland Children's Museum with National Conference of Christians and Jews 1993 with WVIZ and 11 community organizations.

Shaker Towers, A Diverse Environment.

VISUAL IMAGES

Don Harvey: *Bad Water*, Cleveland Museum of Art, 2008.

Caydie Heller: *Shaker Lakes*, photograph, from "Preserving Our Natural Heritage", Shaker Life Feb/Mar 2012.

Lori Kella: *Blue Ore Boat*, archival pigment print, 2013, 30x30.

Susan Klarreich: *Heron,* photograph at Shaker Lakes.

Michael Loderstedt: in consonance with Urban Evidence; Contemporary Artists Reveal Cleveland, 1996.

Michaelangelo Lovelace: "78th Street and Nowhere" 1994. "These Urban Streets" 2013. painting.

Chris Pekoc: *Traversing Lake Erie,* mixed media, SPACES, 2009.

Judy Rawson: *Detail of printing press at Morgan Conservancy*, photograph, 2015.

Randall Tiedman: *Night's Speechless Carnival* courtesy of Kokoon Arts Gallery (see Douglas Max Utter essay).

Douglas Max Utter: *Cleveland Rain*, 8ft x 9ft, 2000.

Laila Voss: A *Chaotic Symphony—The Catch-All Net, massive three-part multi-media installation commissioned by MOCA, concurrently shown at CMA and SPACES* in consonance with Urban Evidence; Contemporary Artists Reveal Cleveland, 1996.

CURRICULUM

Danny Hoch, *Towards a Hip Hop Aesthetic: A Manifesto for the Hip-Hop Arts Movement.*

Nancy Murnyak, Architecture Curriculum, John Hay High School (with Judson Kline FAIA).

ARTICLES

Diana Simeon, "Preserving our Natural Heritage", Shaker Life, Feb/March 2012.

WEBSITES

Links to relevant institutions and organizations can be found in CAN Journal, or at this book's website on ATBOSH.com

People Known, Taught, Mentored, & Loved:

Doris, Donald, Amy, Al, Gerda, Jud, Lane, Lori, Foteni, Nancy, Jim, Gladys, Jean, Jack, Brian, Frank, Masumi, Maggie, Jack, Abbie, Linda, Ona, Bill, Tim, Henry, Foteni, Sam, Carol, Paul, Zelma, Sollace, Julie, Joellen, Joe, Sari, Renee, Henry, Connie, Michael, Claudia, Kristin, Carl, Martha, Eve, Ernestine, Gene, Leon, Johnnie, H.C., Carroll, P.K., Alenka, Frances, Kathleen, Mary, Jerry, Joyce, Tom, Lester, Geri, Donna, Foster, Malcolm, Bonnie, Maureen, Jill, David, Bob Sr., Madelein, Mueller, HM Ruth, Karl, Robert, Kathy, Diane, Rachel, Jared, Jane, Louis, Jim, Chris, Jennifer, Darlyn, Pat ,Suzanne, Marie, Judith, Enid, Sabine, Fr. Timothy Buyansky OSB, Neal, Sara, Pam, Denise, Sherman, Alec, Adam, William, Katharine, Katie, Andrew, Mary, Kay, MareyJoyce, Ray, Kevin, Marsha, Tonya, Mark, Jurgen, Alan, Maria, Brian, MaryBeth, Noelle, Jordan, Gala, Charles, Diane, Ruth, Valerie, Dean, Lew, Joanie, Melissa Hunter Jane, Susan, Deborah, Norman, Eric, Margaret Gail, Ellen, Deena, Jan, Laura, Gloria, Dick, Joanne, Heather, Ted, Nikki, Sally, Karen, Tom, Robin, Lucy, Terri, Herb, Natalie, Lainie, Shivani, Jack, Marilyn, Debbie, Marjorie, Kim, Dave, Maria, Dale, Trudy, Grafton, Darlene, Kathryn, Barbara, Ann, Suzanne, Michael, Oliver, Sari, Felton, Ryan, Sarah, Harvey, Liz, Dan, Fred, Elizabeth

PLACES Presentations Programs

Cleveland State University
Case Western Reserve University
Baker-Nord Center for the Humanities
Laura and Alvin Siegal Lifelong Learning Program
LNOCA Meeting
Avon Schools
St Edwards
St. Martin de Porres
Parma city Schools (Media Specialist) 7-12
East High School (CPS)
Garfield Hts. High School
Hudson City Schools
Benedictine High School
Cleveland Public Schools
Hawken
Laurel
Hathaway Brown
University School
Western Reserve Academy
John Hay High School
Shaker Heights Public Schools (all levels)
Cleveland Public Library and Branches
Independent Libraries
Cuyahoga County Public Libraries

End Notes
Artifacts at 60 Years

As a family, we shared soul experiences away from home — in San Francisco with holocaust survivor Gloria Lyons, in Kansas, at The Land Institute, preserving the prairie, examining our environment through Man and His Land, up the mountains of Colorado, or along the Connecticut River and the New England greenery.

As a child, I thought the soul of the city lived in the echoes of our voices, or as we honked our horn under the graceful Schweinfurth bridges over Rockefeller Park. Or, in the Spring smell as we passed the arched lilacs at the corner of Euclid Avenue and East Boulevard. Or, with the engineer (a magician) who opened, turned and closed the bridge we went over the Cuyahoga River on our way to the West Side. All of this is still the soul of the city. It sits in our "being".

Places age with memory. Each day the challenge is to search, to seek, to taste the past, drink to the future triggered by a word, a call, a scene, an image. Do we answer, respond, hang up, talk, or wonder?

Memories feed our soul. A Color stays. Your mind goes awry. It is hard to concentrate. Like ice cream oozing from a cone, the day melts with it. Plaques on the buildings hint history. Touch history, Remember. Then it's gone again. The orchestra plays perfectly. Remember. Then it disappears. Our mind wanders away.

Literature feeds our soul. Re-reading molds the cushion on the chair, the pillow, our dreams.

Holding truth is hard. People are truth. Our lives are filled with truth. Hang on. This book is about mindful people — the soul of this city.

The truthsayers. The aging wine. They capture importance. They make us people. They make us see and think. They are the fabric of place. Help us know who we are.

WHEREABOUTS:

We decided to sell our Shaker Towers condo of 31 years. The opportunity of moving to a brand new state-of-the art Assisted Living floor at JUDSON (take a look on Internet) seemed timely. It took hold quickly when we made one phone call to see how hard it might be to sell our place and our friend returned our call by saying they wanted to buy it. They lived in the building and wanted ours for its view and larger size. BINGO –

We spent wonderful early years in Kansas and San Francisco, and traveled many places over 61 years as you know, but this move is significant in a couple of ways.

We are still in the neighborhood!
This move is:
- A mile from where N was born and across the street from where her parents lived (Cedar Glen)!
- ½ mile from where she lived for years — (top of Cedar Hill next to Nighttown; house on Fairmount Blvd.)
- ½ mile from where J and N lived for 54 years (Warrington; Shaker Blvd.)
- 6 minutes from Shaker Towers, our 11th floor condo where we lived for 31 years
- A place that Jim has had a long relationship having renovated the building.

We find two rooms at this new assisted living area designed by Herman Gibans Fodor (now HDS Architects) perfect for us. Our artwork, books, resource papers, plants and furnishings have found new "homes" with family, friends, non-profit organizations, and libraries through meaningful conversations and visits. While downsizing, we had lots of discussion and visits from family — memorable reunions pre-move — October in Vermont at peak and Thanksgiving at our Shaker Towers home for 31 years.

It was a really exciting experience. Everything was placed where people wanted them. One last huge portrait of my grandfather was too large for family homes but was wanted by a grandnephew! We knew the painter from Wooster, Ohio also painted Abraham Lincoln several times.

We are thrilled to have our Alcoa Aluminum chess set from the 40s in the chess collection of the Cleveland Public Library, our iconic Saarinen womb chair inherited from my father in the new home of the Director of the

Cleveland Institute of Art, our Jenneret (Corbusier) chairs in the gallery of CIA, Jim's living room table at the Cleveland Public Library, books at libraries all over town and our "children's" books in the library where our children went to elementary school.

So we are here. People ask how we keep busy. What we look like etc. Imagine our old place…reds abounding, 500 CD or DVDs, now on I-PAD and computer, about 30 works of art, several hundred books – an environment to keep us very happy. Food good, several old friends, and many new ones, 24/7 assistance when needed, all located a stone's throw from University Circle and planned bus transport to events downtown. We have been to the Cleveland Museum of Art, SPACES, Transformer Station, Cleveland Orchestra, ChamberFest Cleveland, Groundworks and more. We are involved in planning programs and exhibitions here at JUDSON and have worked in the art therapy studio. Right for us!

SUMMER 2017

"So what do you do all day?" a recurring inquiry from old friends and neighbors. The sun is almost twinkling goodbye to a beautiful summer day in Cleveland Heights in the old area just above the city. The trees are thick with green; the windmill on the roof of a nearby building is quiet. It is peaceful now in this very busy place.

In our first six months, we have happily adjusted to assisted living; (see judsonpark.com) gathering the mighty and precious resources of the people who live here and those who work here. We join those who have given up their cars on a bus that has taken us to museums, concerts, exhibitions, lectures all over the city. In the good auditorium here, we have heard about the solar eclipse and how to observe it properly from the best place...our own front yard. One can join informal conversation and serious discussions. We have fine and folk music and band concerts from students and oldsters. Never thought of yoyo and its challenges if one is really serious about it. Learned all about it at our age. The pianos on each floor are in action several times a week (on the phone today the customer service person on the line wanted to come see what I was hearing!).

And we are surrounded by generous green and colorful gardens, elegant brick and stone houses and the fun of watching restoration and preservation. There is something here for every culture, every mind, background and preference. And history is embedded in this place of peace. Personal histories in the forefront: everyone takes pride as the 104 year-old master gardener picks dead leaves from the huge colorful pots of flowers on the patio or the master ceramist brings his iconic work for an exhibition here.

My history is certainly eclectic — now full circle as I get involved with the programming, and Jim attends men's discussion group and has new time for reading. Could not believe that the mail today from the new president of Sarah Lawrence College took me back to the beginning of this book. She describes the challenges facing American higher education and the need for the college to shape a future facing these challenges. The theme of her inauguration is "Democracy and Education" taken from John Dewey's 1916 book whose concerns were influential in shaping the founding philosophy of the college almost century ago. A phone call tells me that The City Club of Cleveland will recognize the Samuel Oscar Freedlander Memorial Forum this October as they feature Floyd Abrams, iconic lawyer and brilliant thinker and activist on the subject of Free Speech. One couldn't have guessed that I would look into the windows of the apartment building across the street that was my first home.

WHO WE ARE — WHERE WE LIVE
Shaker Square / Buckeye area

Brick by brick, store by store, story by story. Lucky me. I have been "engaged" to The Square since childhood through food, filmmaking, interviewing and programming. Is it best for an evening walk with the couples, the dog walkers, the skateboarders or memories of Arabica's for coffee and conversation, Tassi's and Shaker Square Beverage for special food and wine, Anna Polshek for grown-up dresses or children's clothes at Helen Hale? Is it best to remember one of the first tent art shows in town? As a 'kid" I went bowling, stopped at Miller Drugs for ice cream, experienced my first solo rapid rides to downtown.

And mid-life I helped organize and advocate for the repairs of a crumbling past to the future and present we know. My children were among the last to choose a toy at Clark's Restaurant, pick up an afternoon pastry a Hough Bakery or shop at the music store. I have been a Friend of Shaker Square since its inception. The children have gone on to live in four different states, missing the community connectedness of the Saturday mornings at the loyal gatherings at the food stalls of the North Union Farmer's Market and the social consciousness of the owners of Edwin's. These are heartfelt and unique.

The glamour and romanticism of Balaton's at their original spot on Buckeye with violins playing at the table to dinner at the restaurant the night my first book was accepted for publication by Praeger Press. The telephone operator armed with the old-fashioned plug-in system at Moreland Courts was the queen of information in touch with her building residents on the affairs of the square regarding their personal needs – heat—when to turn on an off – and deliveries from the drug store, cleaners, and grocers. Those seem like ancient history when elegance reigned and city leaders lived at the square to escape the soot of the town and the advantage of the rapid transit.

As Shaker Square began to believe in its importance as a portal to the eastern suburbs, to the national model of integration of Shaker Heights, and its wonderful core location and city population mix, it changed its services: DAVE's grocery store, foods ranging from popcorn to many fine restaurants –ethnic, delis, and serious French cooking. It started to embrace the contingent location of Larchmere full of boutiques, good food and where the major bookstore finally rested.

Fun stories abound. People meeting their boy and girl friends there, women going into labor at the movie theatre, and families sitting on the lawn for band concerts. One time, when interviewing residents or visitors, an older resident insisted that she shopped at HMO Schwartz (FAO Schwartz) and a man said he was the "mayor" of Shaker Square.

I lived on the eastern edge of the square in Shaker Towers condominium for 31 years. While living on Warrington at Onaway Rds., prior to that for over 20 years, our family lived through the process of integrating Shaker Heights — they went to both Onaway and Moreland Schools which gave us insight and perspective on what all of this meant. Current national exhibitions at the NY Public Library and stories in major newspapers like the NY Times verify this as still a national model. This only laid the groundwork for a lifelong attitude.

Later, as empty nesters we chose to live on the 11th floor of the tallest building on the east side. We could look at the lake, see the storms come in and out, pretend we were in Central Park because of all of the greenery and continue our belief in the square as a haven for the city's populations. Shaker Towers was constructed in 1948 to allow populations that had not been allowed at Moreland Courts under the covenants of the Van Sweringens to live at the square in suites as spacious as those at the courts. All of this is true history and to present generations seems a made-up fairy tale. Thus our neighbors were Rabbi Lelyveld, Zelma George, Carl Stokes, Dorothy Fuldheim, who broke the barriers. The population mix has remained to this day and as other properties followed national regulations the building stands tall in social leadership, a characteristic of Shaker Square.

We had known Fred Schmidt for over 25 years and had been commissioning art from local artists to celebrate birthdays and anniversaries. We decided to engage Fred for a special double celebration on the millennium. This lyrical work in red celebrated our 45th wedding and anniversary and Jim's 70th birthday. Fred came over to discuss what we had in mind early in 1999 and he had about a year to create it. He arrived in September declaring it "his best work yet". We have loved this piece that stands sentry on our coffee table in the living room area of our apartment — a cannot-miss part of our surroundings. It's a cheerful soaring welcome to all who visit.

Dancing to 45/70 (commission for celebrations) 1999.
Fred Schmidt, Sculptor

Shaker Towers

Gibans Judson Apartment

Addendum:
Voices from the Community

Barbara Robinson keynote at "On and Off the Wall" event at the Cleveland Public Library, 2015

In today's consideration of where we are and where we're going, I want to go farther back to what was a pivotal period to me in the review of where we are and of how we got there.

I cannot remember a time in which I was not a believer in the importance of the arts; however, as far as morphing into being an active advocate, I was a naive, non-practitioner until I became involved in public sector funding for the arts. I was actively "pushed" into the pool when, Jesse Helms, Senator from North Carolina, took, as a platform for his political ambitions and advancement, a proposal to eliminate the National Endowment for the Arts by preventing its federal funding.

His denial of funding was based upon two assumptions: A personal prejudice, I believe, regarding the funding of recent grants made to artist whom he considered indecent, unworthy of public funding. Feelings attributed motivations to personal issues of

Jesse Helms regarding race and sexuality. The second major influence on his choice of battleground was his perception of the national arts community as one that would have little impact or ability to obstruct because it was widely dispersed, politically inactive and unorganized.

The National Endowment for the Arts could not lobby for itself.

However, the challenge of a response was taken up by the National Association of State Arts Agencies (NASAA). The Washington-based service organizations for States Arts Agencies that existed in each of the 50 states and territories; NASAA, as it was called, took up the challenge first by analysis of funding authority (Congress) elected by votes and financial contributions from state constituencies, on the premise that when elected, these representatives were expected to represent the interests of their states.

At that time, as the Chair of NASAA, along with its Advocacy Committee Chair, Tom Schorgl, who was a member of my NASAA Board as the Director of the Indiana Arts Commission, took up the challenge.

Tom and BBSR targeted regional meetings of SAAs across Federal officials to defeat Jesse Helms' initiative. (If for no other reason than to safeguard federal monies coming from the NEA to the states).

The success of our efforts joined with the activities of other like-minded individuals and organizations is one of the prime examples I can give you of the value of the arts and artists as advocates.

We can't predict challenges of similar magnitude (or even of lesser magnitude); yet looking at Helms' response, there's been a mind-set change in both funding of individual artists and the artist's role in advocacy and affecting change.

The results of this rude awakening had the effect of a pebble being dropped into a pond. One of the most striking examples was and is most visible in Ohio. In the 80's and 90's, leading the nation in its reputation in creatively developing programs to fill the gap in funding throughout the artistic infrastructure was the Ohio Arts Council. Ohio was the leader of the national arts council movement. At that time, most recognized for its dedicated programs to support arts and arts organizations in their communities. Through our state, the Arts Council was the first to dedicate programs to fund substantially individual artists and do the same for other related concerns to regarding minority artists and minority-operated organizations, adding evidence of a defined outreach program in guidelines for applications for Operating Grants and instituting International Exchanges to widen artist's opportunities for increasing audience experiences, and to develop reputations outside of the state. (There was a "How To" manual published on International Exchanges and distributed to other colleagues in the State Arts Council field). All of these resonate today by experiences in Cleveland, mainly initiatives undertaken by CPAC, the Cleveland Foundation, Cleveland Arts Prize, Cuyahoga County — even Playhouse Square and SPACES, as examples.

The NEA was saved, with the immediate goals being reached through advocacy. As I mentioned, the challenges of the future are hard to predicate, but not the continuing role of advocacy.

Advocacy is Ad-Voce.

Voce — Voice of the artists such as yours, is in your work itself. The expression of needs, of value, of sensibility, perception, whether it is individually internal or externally oriented.

As — addresses that the community also has need, values, goals, and where the artists move with mutual respect and understanding in whatever voices exist to move together into the future to where you, plural, want to be.

In order for this to happen, it is not only to give voice, but also to listen to the voice of the public to join the discussion of issues. This demands of the artists and art, not to be insular, but to participate — to be active where decisions are being made — whether it be through PTO's, CDC's, foundations, community planning, building authorities, etc. Advocacy is value and belief-based with a strategy that is goal-oriented. Success is measured by a mutual goal being reached through mutual understanding, engagement as to where you have to be to get where you want to be. This also works with relationships with potential funders, who are today increasingly concerned with societal issues. This is not a "touch-y feel-y" undertaking, but is realpolitik.

Advocacy is, in this sense, not everyone's cup of tea, but look to today's presentations and think of where they are — or where they would have been — without some bodies making some of outside bodies advocates for the inclusion of arts and artists, and then think about what needs to be considered in light of achieving change for the future.

Artists must be advocates for their own role in today's society. No one else is going to do it for you.

Part of the Whole: Participate, have a seat at the table where decisions are made.

Participate in other's values, **understand** their values, and **appeal** to their values. Engage others. Mutual understanding. Attend appropriate meetings.

Voices

Kathleen Cerveney

When I was a girl, I had dreams of being a dancer, a concert pianist, and actress. But there were no opportunities to pursue these dreams in the tiny suburb southwest of Cleveland where my family lived. By the time I reached high school, though, I could get an RTA bus downtown and I spent my Saturdays up on the third floor of the Cleveland Public Library, where I devoured Dance Magazine, Old Vic recordings of Shakespeare plays. I sat in the Eastman Reading Garden listening to the classical music they piped out there in the summertime, and I'd walk down those great marble stairs to the lower level, where glass cases held treasure of the Art Museum's extension collection. The library opened the world of the arts to me.

All the arts have been a fascination for me all my life and if you asked me, I could not choose a favorite. Back then I could never have imagined that my life's work would involve me in serving and supporting every one of the arts that I loved so dearly. So it is with amazement, delight and deep, deep gratitude that I have been given this chance through the remarkable and unique institution that is the Cleveland Foundation.

The Foundation's commitment to the arts doesn't stop with a response to the many grant requests we receive each year. The Cleveland Foundation is committed to proactively advancing the health of the cultural sector itself, to make the arts accessible to the least advantaged in our community, and to develop public policy that validates the arts as a critical element of a civil, sophisticated, and economically robust society. It is a privilege to be a part of that commitment. Receiving the Bergman Prize is a very special honor for me. During his short time with us, I can to know Bob well. He was a passionate and joy-filled change agent willing to step outside the walls of his institution to both serve and lead in the community.

I met Bob almost immediately after he became Director here. We were both at an arts conference in Chicago and just happened to be seated together at lunch. After talking for a while about our respective jobs, he leaned over and whispered, quite conspiratorially to me "I can't believe they are letting me run the Cleveland Museum of Art!" That was Bob, happily sharing the delight he felt in the opportunity ahead.

Looking back now, over more than two decades of my work at the Cleveland Foundation, I have to echo Bob's delighted amazement and say I can't believe the Foundation has let me be a part of its great work here.

I stand in continuous awe of the talent of our artists, many of whom have become dear friends, and some of whom are being honored here tonight — and for the past 54 years by the Arts Prize. I am incredibly proud and grateful to the dedicated patrons of the arts whose generosity has made Cleveland a cultural center that punches far above its weight. This is a remarkable city we live in, isn't it?

I want to thank the artists, the arts leaders, the cultural institutions that make my life richer than I ever thought it could be. I thank Deena for being a committed colleague and partner with me in this work — it is a joy to share this award with her.

I must, of course, thank the Foundation for whatever small part I have been privileged to play in supporting the arts here. Finally, and most sincerely, I thank the Arts Prize for this humbling and deeply meaningful honor.

Robert Conrad

What is the most important aspect of WCLV, Cleveland's classical music station? The answer is, that after 55 years as of November 1st, 2017, it is still here, broadcasting classical music 24/7. Founded in 1962 by C. K. "Pat" Patrick and Robert Conrad, the station's programming is as much as what it was on the day the FCC granted the transfer of license from the previous owners. This was pioneer time in FM. Only one-third of the households in Northeast Ohio had radios that received FM signals. And there were no car radios with FM.

However, three events helped WCLV survive its early years. One, the Catholic Diocese rented the station's sub-carrier to broadcast school curriculum programs into the Diocesan school classrooms. Second, in 1964, Cleveland Trust (now KeyBank) purchased a five-night-a-week, one-hour of symphonic music that the station named "Symphony at Seven". Now beginning its 64th year, it is still supported by KeyBank. The program is the longest running sponsored radio program in Cleveland. Then in 1965, the Cleveland Orchestra chose WCLV to produce and distribute the concerts of the ensemble. And today, the Orchestra is heard twice a week on the station, and the series of national broadcasts is the longest-running orchestra program in the nation. Over the years, WCLV has made a conscious effort to air programs, live and delayed, of the multitude of other musical and arts organizations in Northeast Ohio — from the Cleveland Institute of Music, Cleveland State University, Baldwin Wallace University, Oberlin College, The Music School Settlement, ChamberFest Cleveland, to Quire Cleveland and many others.

In 1990, there were 90 commercial classical radio stations. Then in 1996, Congress re-wrote the Telecommunications Act, which at the time restricted the number of radio stations that a given company could own. The new version lifted the restriction and thus began a feeding frenzy of station sales with prices for radio stations reaching unimaginable heights. Today in 2017, there are only seven commercial classical music stations left, although there are numerous public stations airing the format. Several commercial classical stations were purchased by public stations in order that the classical programming could continue — WQXR, New York; WCRB, Boston; KDFC, San Francisco; and KING in Seattle.

The stockholders of WCLV began to wonder about the future of WCLV. They wanted the classical format to continue as the station had become a valuable institution in the community. So on July 3, 2001, they entered into a complicated deal which traded the 95.5 frequency for 104.9, added an AM station to the company, and received a comfortable return on investment. Four years later, the company that sold the

AM station to WLCV bought it back, with the resulting finances that protected WCLV during the 90's recession.

Over the next decade, Cleveland's public television station WVIZ, and public radio station WCPN, merged to form "Ideastream" and built combined facilities on Playhouse Square in downtown Cleveland. They asked WCLV to move in with them. Prodded by the Cleveland Foundation, WCLV decided that the future of WCLV could be secure if the station became a part of "Ideastream". On December 10, 2010, WCLV moved into new facilities in the Idea Center, the home of WVIZ and WCPN; and on January 1, 2013, the stock of WCLV was donated to "Ideastream", and the station became the nation's newest public radio station.

Pamela Eyerdam

The Cleveland Public Library was established in 1869. One of its most important benefactors was John Griswold White, who was a prominent Cleveland lawyer, library board member, patron, book lover, and a world-renowned chess research collector of the twentieth century. His love of books and chess was a perfect combination to build one of the most unique collections that still exists in an American public library. His legacy continues through his book collection and endowment at the Cleveland Public Library.

Mr. White was born in Cleveland on Lakeside Avenue in 1845, just blocks away from what was to be the building of Main Library. Main Library opened in 1925 and was one of the structures of the original Daniel Burnham *Cleveland Mall Plan of 1903*. Mr. White was well-educated and enjoyed reading books at an early age. He was admitted to the Ohio State Bar, graduated in

1865, and was a brilliant young lawyer who specializes in municipal law. He became a loyal board member of the Cleveland Public Library and donated his vast collection of books and established a generous endowment which is still active today.

As a progressive, Mr. White was committed to build a collection that would support the education of the Cleveland community. Topics included chess, folklore, and orientalia (books about the customs and religions of the Middle Far East). Since Cleveland is a multilingual community, there are books written in over 50 languages and over 100 dialects. The Cleveland Public Library continues John G. White's mission as being the "*People's University*", the center of learning for a diverse and inclusive community. Its vision is to be the driving force behind a powerful culture of learning that will inspire Clevelanders from all walks of life to continually learn, share, and seek out new knowledge in ways that are beneficial to themselves, their community, and the world.

John G. White Collection at the Cleveland Public Library. Photograph courtesy of the Cleveland Public Library.

Portrait of John G. White.
Photograph courtesy of the Cleveland Public Library.

Chess set in the John G. White Collection at the Cleveland Public Library. Photograph courtesy of the Cleveland Public Library.

Go West, Young Woman

Ann Klotz

I am not Clevelander. Born and raised on the East Coast, I moved to Cleveland to run an extraordinary school for girls in 2004.

"Go West, young woman," my father teased.

Two of my best friends had grown up in the 216 — one in Shaker, the other in Cleveland Heights. Laurel, the school that has chosen me as its leader, was exceptional; it was the right opportunity, the right moment. So, my husband and I packed up our New York City apartment and headed west. No wagon or trunks. We moved our two daughters, baby son, elderly cat, agreeable dog, and hermit crab into a real house — a lovely home on the grounds of the school with a kind of Hobbit front door, perfect for Halloween.

I had been rooted in a different state, my great-grandfather the patriarch of a distinguished Philadelphia family. Me relatives rest in flat white rows in the cemetery of the Church of the Redeemer in Bryn Mawr — generations neatly arranged. My husband's family, Jewish, has no such history. Theirs is a more traditional immigrant story: refugees fleeing *pogroms* in Poland, assimilated Berlin Jews fleeing *Kristlenacht*. While I kept my own name, I wanted our children to have my husband's name, to carry it forward with them.

Cleveland was a new beginning for our family, and though coming here was a move I sought, change challenged us. In my old school, I was a known quantity. I enjoyed a great deal of social capital. I understood the subtleties of my school's culture. Here, as Headmistress, allegedly in charge and omniscient, I felt brand new and vulnerable. Every element of our life was unfamiliar. I couldn't turn on lights in the school because I didn't know where the switches were. We didn't know where to go for pizza or Chinese good; we drove rather than walked to the supermarket. Our little dog pranced into a fenced backyard instead of needing to be taken out on a leash. The hermit crab gave up the ghost almost immediately. Our elderly cat yowled sadly at walls, the changes simply too dramatic for her. We struggled to put names on unfamiliar faces. But we had enormous support, encouragement. We had enough money, a job; our family was intact. We learned that Cleveland's history is entwined with immigration, with the power of the city's industrial past. I considered how many questions real immigrants must want to ask to find their way, to pretend knowledge they may not possess. Thankfully, we knew the language, had access to phone and email to my family and friends on the East Coast. I empathized with those from earlier eras as well as contemporary immigrants who had to leave all they knew. Even with Google Maps thirteen years later, it's still disconcerting not to know one's way. Our move asked me to conjure my pioneer spirit. We all tried to summon a willingness to leap, trusting that the net would appear.

When we arrived at our new home, halfway up the stairs, we hung a friendship quilt made for a lost relative of mine from a much earlier generation. Dating back to the 19th century, its bright bits of silk and velvet are intricately embroidered with unfamiliar names. I wonder about the quilt's owner. Did she cherish this piece from her past? Did she head West as we did? Isn't Cleveland the Western Reserve of Ohio? I spin stories about her journey into uncharted terrain, ponder her path, her life, give myself over to not knowing and feeling kinship all the same. We are, all of us, seeking.

Sabine Kretzschmar

Food Stories

Two separate lives: what is the community life of food bread? Bread from organic sources. Expressing the "soul" of growing and processing of "food" seems to be something so basic. What are treasured objects here? My quick thoughts (not at all polished, just off the top of my head):

As we make bread, I think a lot about where the ingredients come from, where the equipment comes from, who makes it and who buys it. I've only covered a few of those thoughts here. One little story I might add is that we have a few women who make the bread who are Meskhetian Turks, here in this country as political refugees from various places in the former Soviet Union. Making bread is part of their culture, something they learn as young girls. They often say a Muslim prayer before they shape the bread. I think one way of exploring the soul of bread may be to look at what goes into one loaf. We make a batch of bread every Saturday called "Homegrown Whole Wheat". All of the grains — wheat and oats — are organically grown and milled in Northeast Ohio by the Stutzman Family. Monroe and Martha Stutzman are a young Amish couple in their 30's. We visited their mill near Mount Hope, Ohio, which is powered by natural gas and the sun. An icehouse keeps the cooler at 50 degrees during the summer. The primary milling machine is a handmade, steampunkish-looking behemoth, with some parts over a century old and others brand new. While they may seem old fashioned in the ways that Amish are, they also are savvy business people, who keep up with the latest trends of ancient grains and gluten-free products, catering to their upscale farmers market customers. They also insisted on visiting us when we began our business relationship. We mix the dough and it takes forever to rise, as is the case with whole grain breads. It is baked on out six-ton, stone-lined, steam-injected oven imported from Italy. The ingredients may be local, but this oven is made for bread. Through bread, we have had the privilege to get to know a few different communities in the area. Our Homegrown Whole Wheat attracts a type of person who looks for healthy, organic, local alternatives. They are typically educated, affluent women who are very thoughtful about what they eat. Or for another example, we have authentic Irish Soda Bread that serves the huge Irish community in Lakewood. Our Rustic Italian has been adopted by the large Romanian community (our bread is used for their famous Saint Mary's fish fries during Lent). We are often told by heavily accented people that our bread is just like what they had in Romania.

Elinor Polster

In 1921, before Chester Avenue was even thought of, my father-in-law Norman Polster and his partner Jake Sogolowitz built a 51-suite apartment building on 97th Street in the middle of where Chester Avenue would be. Of course, no one knew Chester Avenue would be constructed there. The apartment was name "Traybird", combining the first names of the two men's wives. When the Cleveland city government decided to build Chester Avenue, they asked Norman Polster and Jake Sogolowitz to move the Traybird. Norman Polster hired a crew which was able to move the building to its permanent site on the Southwest-corner of 97th and Chester. It took a week and all suites were fully occupied. The city paid Norman Polster for the costs of the move, but he was responsible for the move. Over time, the Traybird became one of the first integrated apartment buildings in Cleveland. My family owned the Traybird until we sold it to the Cleveland Clinic in 1986. We hoped the Clinic would use it, perhaps as a Nurses' residence, but they tore it down to make parking lot. Now the lot is under construction for a new Clinic building. My family asked for the cornerstone of the Traybird building when it was being torn down. The cornerstone now resides in the garden of my son, Dan Polster.

P. K. Saha

There was a significant moment concerning the history of poetry in Cleveland in 1962. In that year of crisis between the U.S.A. and Cuba, a group of Cleveland poets gathered near the lagoon near the Cleveland Museum of Art and read Poems for Peace before a large audience. The leader of the poets' group was Mac Hammond. I, P. K. Saha, was among the poets who recited poems in various languages. Unknown to us, one of the persons in the large audience was Cyrus Eaton, prominent business figure on the national and international scene. I was told by an associate of Mr. Eaton that he had written about that poetry reading by the lagoon in his memoir.

FRIENDS OF SHAKER SQUARE
now SHAKER AREA DEVELOPMENT CORPORATION

Starting its existence in 1976 with a Board of Directors consisting of 45 members (this large board was in order to involve as many interested neighbors as possible), Friends of Shaker Square (now known as Shaker Square Area Development) has been influenced by many hundreds of Shaker Square area residents from close Cleveland and Shaker Heights neighborhoods, who have served on the Board, formed committees to take on the multiple tasks that were needed to help stabilize the Square and develop a vision for its future health. A few of the many who have been the most heavily involved over the last 40 years are:

- Cary Straffon/Arden — Founder and 1st President of FOSS
- Caryn Foltz — 2nd President and coordinator of Sh. Sq. physical improvements
- Joan Houghton — led the establishment of Shaker Square Historic District
- Charlotte Cowan — organized art shows on the Square
- Tom & Joanne Adler — Joanne started "A Very Square Affair" annual fundraiser
- Donita Anderson — President, North Union Farmers Market
- Jon Forman —Shaker Cinemas
- Jim & Nina Gibans — (Jim is a Past President)
- Keily & Nancy Cronin
- Charles Beard —
- William Baird — Current President in 2018
- Harry Broder — Past President
- Tom Campbell — Past President
- Jeff Jeney — Past President
- Ted & Beverly Mason

- Keith White
- Margaret Mitchell
- Walter Kelly (former Mayor of Shaker Hts.)
- Jack & Marilyn Bialosky
- Jean Gaede
- Richard Gildenmeister
- Michael Benjamin
- Polly Bruner
- Jeanne Conway
- Laura Berick
- Susan & Tony Troia — Susan is a Past President
- Jim Neville — Past President
- Carol Lowenthal — Past President and Founding Editor of The Connection
- Jeanne Shatten — Past President
- Joanna VanOosterhout — Past President
- Loretta Quade — Past President
- Sandy Hertz — Past President
- Tom Starinsky — Past President
- George Palda — Past President
- Betty Ostew
- Donna Cornett
- Jan Wallace
- Michael Shinn
- Martin Kolb
- Lee Trotter
- Lynn Alfred
- Stanley Jaros — 1st Executive Director
- Reid Robbins — long time Executive Director
- Hanna Fink — former Executive Director
- Catherine Merritt — former Executive Director
- Jane Campbell — former Executive Director
- Joseph Mazzola — former Executive Director
- Greg Staursky — current staff and Manager of SHAD's office building
- Carole Grady — former staff 1939-2005 — Office Manager/Bookkeeper
- Jalene Pardon — former staff (2005-2016) Office Manager/Bookkeeper

- Chris King — long time editor of The Connection Newspaper
- Katherine Kay — former editor of The Connection Newspaper
- Kristen Romito — current editor of The Connection Newspaper
- Larry Albert — past Owner Shaker Square

Rose Ironworks and a Family Story

My first visit to Rose Ironworks was as a young child, when Martin (the founder) had hurt himself in an industrial accident, taking his severed fingers to my father for their reconstruction — which worked. My relationship to Rose Ironworks connected later to teachers and students and with the more recent Rose family members still in command, and very visible to the Cleveland public through the recent Jazz exhibit at the Cleveland Museum of Art. The Rose Ironworks were literally all over Cleveland throughout the ages — in institutions, homes, and businesses.

Railing For The Cleveland Play House, ca. 1927. Rose Iron Works, Inc. (American, Cleveland, est. 1904). Its medium is wrought iron, brass. This railing for the Cleveland Play House reflects mid-18th century French rococo taste.

"Muse with Violin Screen", 1930. Rose Iron Works, Inc. (American, Cleveland, est. 1904). Paul Fehér (Hungarian, 1898-1990), designer. Wrought iron, brass; silver and gold plating; 156.2 x 156.2 cm. The Cleveland Museum of Art, On Loan from the Rose Iron Works

Mirror and Console Table, ca. 1930. Rose Iron Works, Inc. (American, Cleveland, est. 1904). Paul Fehér (Hungarian, 1898-1990), designer. This monumental wrought-iron console and mirror won top prize at the 1931 May Show at the Cleveland Museum of Art, though it remained unsold in the Rose Iron Works studio as the Depression took hold.

List of Poems

- Sustainability
  - Nina Freedlander Gibans
- Listening
  - Nina Freedlander Gibans
- Excerpt from Wild Geese
  - Mary Oliver
- Excerpt from The Cage of Voices
  - Horace Gregory
- A Supermarket in California
  - Allen Ginsberg
- To William Sommer Sunday Morning Apples
  - Hart Crane
- Grey
  - Nina Freedlander Gibans
- for the godfather, daniel thompson (1935-2004)
  - Jeffrey Bowen
- Thoughts on Being Away by January – A Letter to Certain Friends
  - Richard Howard
- Cool Color White
  - Nina Freedlander Gibans

- Jim and Gardens (2 Poems)
    - Nina Freedlander Gibans
- Almost a Find
    - Nina Freedlander Gibans
- The Bridges That Hart Crane Left
    - Nina Freedlander Gibans
- A Conversation
    - Nina Freedlander Gibans
- On the Fine Arts Garden, Cleveland
    - Russell Atkins
- The Revenge of Cleveland, A Menu Against Nouvelle Cuisine
    - Ray McNiece
- Revisiting a Work of Art: Lot's Wife
    - Nina Freedlander Gibans

Violette Heymann, 1910. Odilon Redon (French, 1840-1916). Pastel; unframed: 72 x 92 cm (28 5/16 x 36 3/16 in.). The Cleveland Museum of Art, Hinman B. Hurlbut Collection 1976.1926

About the Author

Nina Freedlander Gibans' biography from her 2009 Cleveland Arts Prize Award as a Community Arts Leader.

Peruse Nina Freedlander Gibans' résumé, and it's fairly obvious that she was put on earth to raise everyone's arts awareness. During the past several decades, this arts visionary and assiduous arts advocate has influenced many of northeastern Ohio's cultural institutions or initiatives. Moreover, her comprehensive book, film and website projects represent a priceless archive that will inform generations to come.

Gibans first began to effect positive change in her hometown while majoring in art, literature and music at Sarah Lawrence College in Bronxville, New York. She engaged the national leadership of Young Audiences to start a chapter in Cleveland.

That was just the beginning of an unprecedented career in strategic arts leadership characterized by her uncanny ability to marshal her multiple talents to maximize the impact of each project she develops. She especially likes to bring educational systems, artists, arts organizations and the public and private sector together to provide arts experiences to students of all ages—whether in universities, museums, schools or the community at large.

In other words, Gibans doesn't just start projects: She builds the collaborations necessary to ensure their success and sustainability. Finally, she fully documents the effort, leaving a legacy for others to study and follow.

For example, in the '70s, she launched the Cleveland Area Arts Council and, as executive director, guided its pioneering efforts to enhance the city's urban environment through a variety of public art initiatives, some of which can still be seen in today's cityscape. In 1976, she received the National Arts Management Award from Arts Management magazine for this work. Her book, "The Community Arts Council Movement: History, Opinions and Issues", remains the definitive study of the arts council movement in America.

Many consider her tour de force project to be her role as curator of a series of public forums entitled "Cleveland's Creative Essence, 1900-2000, The Distinctive and the Distinguished," which culminated in her book, "Creative Essence: Cleveland's Sense of Place." Gibans once received a 6 a.m. phone call from the Queen of Jordan inquiring about another of Gibans' books, Children's Museums: Bridges to the Future, based on her experiences as a founders and director of special programs of Cleveland's Children's Museum.

As a 25-plus-year board member and past president of the Cleveland Artists Foundation, she has worked diligently to help the organization achieve its goals of serving as an intellectual force in preserving and telling the remarkable story of the region's artists, past and present.

Her work as a poet and with the community of poets is a major priority. To commemorate the life and contributions of Daniel Thompson (1935–2004), Cuyahoga County's longtime poet laureate, she spearheaded a campaign that saw West Second Street renamed "Daniel's Way." With the support of a Martha Holden Jennings Foundation grant she directed the development of a website on the history of the region's poetry to accompany her "Cleveland Poetry Scenes" project. She has also developed websites on regional architecture and art that feature history, units of curriculum, glossaries, bibliographies and links to other relevant websites.

Working with the Cleveland area schools is always a key component of any project Gibans undertakes. "Research should not just sit on the shelf," Gibans observed. "It should become a vital part of learning for everyone, but specifically for schoolchildren."

In 2008, Gibans received awards from the Cleveland Restoration Society/AIA Cleveland and from the preservation office of the Ohio Historical Society for her curatorial work on "Cleveland Goes Modern: Design for the Home 1930-1970," an exhibition of mid-century modern residential architecture in northeastern Ohio.

One of her greatest influences and sources of inspiration has been her 50-plus-year marriage to architect James D. Gibans, FAIA, retired principal of Herman Gibans Fodor, Incorporated, whom she refers to as a "true ally."

Julian Stanczak's, *Carter Manor*, 1973. Silkscreen, 33" x 16". From the City Canvases project in the 1970s, which Nina spearheaded at the Cleveland Area Arts Council. This piece now greets the Gibans' friends. For the 2018 FRONT International Cleveland Triennial, the mural will be re-created on its original twelve-story building on Prospect Avenue and Ninth Street.